MIND GAMES

poetry Pt today

MIND GAMES

Edited by Suzy Walton

First published in Great Britain in 2001 by Poetry
Today, an imprint of
Penhaligon Page Ltd, Remus House, Coltsfoot Drive,
Woodston, Peterborough. PE2 9JX

© Copyright Contributors 2001

All rights reserved. No part of this publication may be
reproduced, stored in a retrieval system, or transmitted
in any form or by any means, without prior permission
from the author(s).

A Catalogue record for this book is available from the
British Library

ISBN 1 86226 696 4

Typesetting and layout, Penhaligon Page Ltd, England.
Printed and bound by Forward Press Ltd, England

Foreword

Mind Games is a compilation of poetry, featuring some of our finest poets. This book gives an insight into the essence of modern living and deals with the reality of life today. We think we have created an anthology with a universal appeal.

There are many technical aspects to the writing of poetry and *Mind Games* contains free verse and examples of more structured work from a wealth of talented poets.

Poetry is a coat of many colours. Today's poets write in a limitless array of styles: traditional rhyming poetry is as alive and kicking today as modern free verse. Language ranges from easily accessible to intricate and elusive.

Poems have a lot to offer in our fast-paced 'instant' world. Reading poems gives us an opportunity to sit back and explore ourselves and the world around us.

Contents

What Kind Of World?	H Hanson	1
No Return	Kathleen South	2
What Is Dying?	Tony Fuller	3
Wisdom	John E Lindsay	4
Thoughts Of A Senior Citizen	Kenneth Gilmore	5
Santa's Lighthouse	Amanda Clapp	6
Little Baby Bee	Kevin C Dwane	7
When Planets Collide	Chris McIntosh	8
Kisses From Heaven	Raymond J Lever	9
Listen	Christine Williams	10
Winter Warmers	R N Taber	11
Christmas Memories	Sandra Bridgeman	12
My Rocking Horse	Birthe McCabe	13
Kizzened	Val Stephenson	14
When Can I Pray?	Geraldine M Archer	15
Hard Times	David L Waggett	16
Defrosted	Ian Newman	17
Type One Human	Irene Roberts	18
The Harbingers	M Cooper	19
Un-Found Love	Philip Ellison	20
First Poem About Anything	K Glover	21
Computers For The Over 60's	Jonis Pastit	22
War Of Want	Doug Smith	23
The Last Electric Scarecrow	Paul Williams	24
Night Magic	John Rackham	25
Færie Found	John A Mills	26
How	Callum Donnelly	27
Blessing	Marianne Harvey	28
Love's Trials	Patrick Fitzhenry	29
Spike	D G W Garde	30
The Spectacle Brigade	Greta E Bray	31
Love Of A Child	Kevin P S Collins	32
Good Friends	Keith B Osborne	33
Sleep	Barbara Robson	34
Tea Time	Gerry Greaves	35
Venus Fly Trap	Jeremy Jones	36

Broken Dreams	Eileen P Dunn	37
The Patient Nurse	Chrissie McGrew	38
Love And Hate	Roma Davies	39
To My Beloved Children	Winifred Parkinson	40
Come Closer	Alison Fewins	41
A Visitor To The Harvest Festival	Don Barker	42
A Special Gift!	Anna Marie	44
Positive Thinking ~ On Winter	Emma Dronfield	45
Angel	Paul Ingham	46
Christmas Celebration	Elizabeth Myra Crellin	47
The Gift Of Time	Fred Simpson	48
The Magic Of A Home	Margaret Hubball	49
Green	Maria Carmen Lee Costello	50
In Memoriam di Leandro Tintinalli 1910-2000	Anthony Rosato	51
North West	D T Fletcher	52
Squishy And Icky	Mo Bailey	53
SOS	Barbara Young	54
Progress?	Vivian Finlay	56
A Cry For Help	William D Watt	57
I'm Bored!	Darron Furness	58
Bats In The Attic	Jill Darby	59
Tide	Michael Cooper	60
All Children ~ Beware	Louise Stokes	61
God Is With Us	S Peters	62
A Cake Of Peace	Francis Allan Hoggarth	63
The Book Of Love	Maxine Kaye	64
Sad And Blue	Gibby	65
A Question Of Dying	Diana S L Cook	66
The Mouse	J O Coatswith	67
The Trees Speak	Julia Davenport	68
The Greedy Bunny	J E Lovell	69
A Highland Morning	Sally Bosson	70
The Queen Mother	Eileen Pearce	71
You Know Who You Are!	Susie J Burnette	72
History Repeats	Gail Lawson	73
Enemy Awareness	L Iles	74
Turkish Disaster Appeal	M Goat	75

Title	Author	Page
Children Of The World	Mary Neill	76
The Cave	Stephanie Munro	77
Blue Guitar	Paul Kelly	78
What Is It?	Anita Bricknell	79
Alfriston Scene	G Carpenter	80
The Dome (We Actually Went There)	P Davies	81
Nemesis	A M Woolman	82
All Of Me . . .	Janice Walpole	83
Broken Trust	Anne Wheble	84
A Wild Night	Helen Phillips	85
Boys . . .	Elaine Spence	86
Harvest	Jemma Towler	87
New Babies	Christine Edwards	88
Bats	Kenneth Berry	89
To You Dear Mother	Kirsten Cassidy	90
The Alphabet	Lillian Jones	91
Little Angels Nursery	Julia Donaldson	92
Apple Tree	Chloe Loughran	93
But Where Are My Flowers?	Stephanie Lynn Teasdale	94
The Seaside	Joan Lipman	95
Dark As Night	Marion Lee	96
A Few Characters	Keith L Powell	97
The Driving Test	Bess Langley	98
Raindrops	Gloria Thorne	100
The Glider	Joyce Lane	101
Without You	Janet Clayton	102
Tea For Thought	Marion Moylan	103
Life's Tapestry	Valerie J Owen	104
My Ideal Man	Sandra Ann Marshall	105
No Answers	Paul W Fleming	106
A New Life	Lilian Day	107
A Good Friend	John Nelson	108
Paddy's One True Love	Anthony K Philpot	109
High-Rise Neighbour	Emelie Buckner	110
My Thoughts!	Marianne White	111
Carpet Maker	Christine Laverock	112
A Magnetic Charm	Janet Weatherhead	113

Generosity	A W Day	114
The Blot	J R Hirst	115
Evensong ~ Winchester Cathedral	Eric Ashwell	116
Only To Be With You	Leisha	118
The Face	Marcus Tyler	119
Jessica	A Griffin	120
Village Dreams	Angela Pritchard	121
To Spring	Trev Taylor	122
The Awakening	Pamela Garnell	123
Perfect Melody	Mollie D Earl	124
For A Son Killed In A Car Crash	John K Coleridge	125
Meeting Of The Minds	Philip Newton	126
Reflections	Laura Stinchcombe-Sorrell	127
The Unappreciated Friend	Laura Susan Arnold	128
Homesick	Leonie Smith	129
Journeys	J Bowman	130
War-Time Memories	Michael Dennis	131
The Beauty Of Islay	Mary Hudson	132
Little Robin Redbreast	Annie McKimmie	133
Afternoon Tea	Peggy Hunter	134
The Sleepers	Janet Cavill	135
The Sky	Nicola Avino	136
The Millennium	Ethel M Crowther	137
Sands Of Time	Edith M Stott	138
Earth's Jewels	Dorothy Morris-Hague	139
Mum's Eye View	Dorothy Knight	140
The Wonders Of My World	Marilyn Campbell	141
Roses	John Kirkham	142
Marking Time	Millie Wade	143
Seasons Of Life	Christine A Smithies	144
Dead To Sleep	Julie Ashpool	145
A Bad Day	Anne Wareing	146
Change	Vivien Holden	147
Noises In The Night	Diana Daley	148
Fish And Chips	Neville Anthony	149
My Monkey	Sylvia Jennings	150
Spring	Gemma King	151

Sidmouth	Amelia Wilson	152
Impression Of St Giles's Church, Cambridge	Helen M Seeley	153
Own Bed	Sarah J Bell	154
Runaway	Wendy Trott	155
Kids	D Tinson	156
Staple Plain	Mary Farrell	157
Life Blood Of Our City	M E Weeks	158
Simple Pleasures	P E Poole	159
Paraphrase For Ann	F Littlewood	160
Puddles	Tom Sage	161

What Kind Of World?

In a world of despair, self-hatred and shame,
it's women and children who suffer the pain.
Forever bombarded with news of these crimes,
yet another rape happened, but only a few lines.

What kind of society revolves around sex,
on TV, in papers, crimes up to our necks.
Another child abused, was it a priest or a dad,
the emotions they must go through, make me so sad.

Fathers, grandads, choir master or uncle,
some men today are a massive carbuncle.
They care not of the damage, living in their den,
the trauma and shame they cause, what's wrong with men?

Look in your mental health wards, those needing long-term care,
coping with drugs and alcohol, emotions lying bare.
Causing us to dissolve like a disprin, and disappear,
damaged kids are damaged adults, whom exist upon fear.

H Hanson

No Return

No act of God
The wrath of war,
That take the lives
Of men by score.

The noise of guns
The angry roar,
A thousand men
Lay on the floor.

To all the mothers
One and all,
Whose sons all heard
The battle call.

You're not alone
Along with me,
With thoughts of how
Things used to be.

Alas, our sons
With us no more,
We wish that they'd
Not gone to war.

The war is over,
Battles won,
But that will not
Bring back our sons.

So mine is just
A simple prayer
God love and keep
Them in Your care.

Kathleen South

What Is Dying?
(Adapted from a text by Bishop Brent)

I stand here, on life's lonely shoreline.
As you leave for a distant terrain.
Like a 'Ship in the night'.
You pass from my sight.
And I know I'll not see you again.

You head for a distant horizon.
Become smaller, as you drift away.
My heart feels so bleak.
There are no words to speak.
Just silence as I stand here and pray.

'They have gone,' someone says, stood beside me.
Gone where? They are still the same size.
With a tear on my cheek.
I still cannot speak.
For the going is all in my eyes.

Standing on some other shoreline.
In a land which is pure and bright.
Others watch across seas.
Where a home-coming breeze.
Will bring the same ship into sight.

Many voices will shout the glad tidings.
As the wind in her sails, softly sighing.
Brings her closer to the shore.
There's rejoicing once more.
No sadness my friend . . . That is dying!

Tony Fuller

Wisdom

Situations and people around you abound
But only a few make impressions profound.
Unfashionable. Unpopular even shunned by the herd
You find there a light commonly shared,
Revelation, a link as you more deeply probe
You peel back each layer under that robe
And what do you find?
All seek to achieve the same in the end
Health and content with faith in a friend.

John E Lindsay

Thoughts Of A Senior Citizen

So many things are treasured more
As time goes on its way ~
Old friends, old times, old memories
All grow dearer day by day.
And that's the way with birthdays
For each time you add one more
Somehow you're still more special
Than you were the year before.
God planned the smallest detail
On the day He formed the earth,
So just as carefully He planned
Each detail of your birth.
He blesses us and fills us
With a joy beyond all measure,
For He considers each of us
A rare and priceless treasure.
There is a path beyond our world
Where God will take our hand
And take us home to live with Him
In His great eternal land.

Kenneth Gilmore

Santa's Lighthouse

Sand beneath my feet,
Hair blowing in the breeze,
Eyes closed, ears listening to the waves.

It waits patiently on the shore
Admiring the view.
A Cyclops eye guiding the bygone sailors.
Little feet pad up the wooden steps,
On tiptoes she peers through the door,
Nothing, but dust and cobwebs.

'So where did he go? Last night when I saw him,
From Lapland to Burnham and back?
Surely he must have a secret hideaway'
She sits on a step and ponders,
Over the hoof prints and sleigh trails in the sand
Maybe it's magic . . .

With the wind in my face
I smile over my fragile memories
Of Santa Claus and his summer retreat!
As the waves chase each other up the beach
The donkeys are on their way home.
The water covering their footprints,
To make way for tomorrow's memories.

Amanda Clapp

Little Baby Bee

A baby bee took flight today
He flew up to the sky
And to his little hive below
He waved and said goodbye

The sun shone bright
On the little mite
As he smiled at the sun
He thought to himself

Look what I can do
I can fly. I can fly
I can soar to the sky
I can do anything I want to

He flew for a time and buzzed aloud
As he danced on every single cloud
He waggled his tail in a cheerful way
His heart was joyful that summer's day

Then searching for hours and hours
To find lots of pretty flowers
And finding one quite soft and pink
Curling up he fell asleep

Kevin C Dwane

When Planets Collide

Many Light Years ago
In a Starburst Galaxy
Two Planets Stood in close proximity
So Distant from one another
Not Knowing
But at a Fire Storm From a Solitary Star
The Quiet Change
Swift as it begun
Inflamed by this Celestial Passion
The Planets begun to Slowly change their orbit
As if Micro secound by Micro secound
Light Years Interchanged Bound for one another
As if in Space and Time
The Planets Glowed
White Hot with Heat
An all consuming
Gravitational Passion Feeding on itself
For a Life Long Companion
Yet this is our Destiny
And Then The Planets Collided
In an all consuming Embrace

And God Called Them Man and Woman

Chris McIntosh

Kisses From Heaven
(Dedicated to my Foster Parents)

Don't cry 'Dear Greta', don't cry anymore,
Though I know you are grieving for the one you adore.
Thank 'God' for his blessings; Ernie's now free from pain,
But don't cry 'Dear Greta', for you'll both meet again.

Don't cry 'Dear Greta', though I know you're apart,
And tears of sorrow are breaking your heart
Try to be brave; for his suffering was cruel,
So don't cry 'Dear Greta', just let 'God's' blessing rule.

Don't cry 'Dear Greta', just try to be strong,
For the one that you loved and cared for so long.
Your heartache will heal; and as long as you pray,
Your tears will dry and your grief fade away.

Don't cry 'Dear Greta', you gave 'Ernie' your best;
But his pain was too much, so 'God' took him to rest.
Just look unto 'Heaven' for the loved one you miss,
A 'Bright Star' will appear, and blow you a kiss.

He'll have many to send ~ but you'll be top of the list,
So don't cry 'Dear Greta' ~ don't cry.

My love to you both ~ Raymond

    Raymond J Lever

Listen

Within the centre of all existence
Lies one tiny spark of creation.
It glitters, shines and dances like a star
In our universal relation.
It sparks and gives life
Creation is its only goal.
Humankind builds in the strife
Instead of listening to the soul.

Christine Williams

Winter Warmers

The hair is greyer
than yesterday;
One more furrow
on the brow;
Sight less clear, than
it used to be;
hearing getting
worse

What now?

A loving heart beats
as yesterday;
No fewer dreams
to inspire;
Looking back, on
a good life;
Glad to chat with
old friends

By the fire

Counting blessings
in the flames;
Seeing, clearly, this
and that mistake;
Happy, just to be
who I am;
If a failure, done
my best

What the heck?

    R N Taber

Christmas Memories

Christmas time a nostalgic time
Takes you way back to the past
When there seemed to be more time
The pace was not so fast

We didn't have a lot you know
All those years ago
But the old sock hung on the bedpost
Brought a magic of its own

In the morning as the dawn broke
Down the bed we all would creep
To see if the old sock had been filled
With some small sweet treats

An apple and an orange
Some nuts a sweet or two
Maybe for the girls a little hairslide
For the boys a small tin flute

We would only have one present
For the girls maybe a doll
For the boys a car or a wooden train
It was all parents could afford

A chicken for Christmas dinner
Then was such a special treat
The stamps and divi Mum saved up
Would do us just a treat

Round the coal fire we would sit
Some carols we would sing
When the Queen's speech came on the radio
We would all listen in.

Sandra Bridgeman

My Rocking Horse

My rocking horse is dapple gray
I ride it almost every day
Sometimes I am a cowboy rounding up the steers
Other days at the rodeos riding for the cheers
My rocking horse and I surely have lots of fun
When the day is over, we are truly done.

Birthe McCabe

*Kizzened**

Eat your dinner . . .
But Da I don't like it
Eat your dinner . . .
Don't waste good food

Went off the school
Jumped over to big desk
You! Ink the blackboard
Was late in from school

Sang 'Annie Laurie'
Wearing pink pom-pom slippers
Is that your sister?
My brother said No!

Eat your dinner . . .
Our John's got what I want
Eat your dinner . . .
There'll be nothing else

Helped with the washing
I turned the mangle
Our Bess caught her finger
Wore bandage for months

Dashed up to Chapel
Promised to be good
Ran all the way home
Yorkshire Pudding today

Eat your dinner . . .
Before it gets kizzened
But Da, that's how I like it
Ma smiled as I ate

slightly dried up

    Val Stephenson

When Can I Pray?

Do I kneel in the morning
For my time with the Lord,
Pray ever so earnestly
Then leave when I'm bored?

Do I stop in the middle
Of a frenzy at noon
Mutter a few hurried words
And I'm off far too soon?

Is my prayer-time at night
When the day is all gone
When I'm frustrated and tired
As I stifle a yawn?

No, I can pray at *all* times
In the morn, noon and night,
If I give God His place
I'll remain in His sight.

Geraldine M Archer

Hard Times

I have been scaling the mountains of madness, and
mingling with the moronic masses, in a mundane
morass of mediocrity.
The stench of ignorance is overwhelming.

Refrain: *'I'd go down on my knees for your black-eyed peas,
do the splits for your hominy grits;
just yell 'Virginia ham' an' honey 'I'm your man', but I'd
sooner sink my teeth into you!*

So I stand on the plain and never complain, and I
watch the coal train; for as long as I sing my refrain,
I'll keep my brain sane!

David L Waggett

Defrosted

She likes me ~ she loves me not,
a four-leafed clover even undermines my plot;
a short-strawed lottery's my lot,
small bricks to build what hopes I've got.

You'd smiled, we spoke, we laughed, you left,
your fingers brushed my elbow like a breath,
a wave, an undercurrent, lightning spark,
on the frosty prism of my arctic heart.

Flight of fancy, wax wings molten near that sun,
a foolish, fevered rush, honeytrap sprung.
Bumblebee's kiss: damned once it's stung;
how tedious adoration has become.

The rainbow bends, endless, beyond view.
Heart worn and torn, beaten, black, blue.
But bruises heal ~ burned fingers, too;
something frost-bitten limbs will never do.

Ian Newman

Type One Human

Yes ~ no. No ~ Why ~ Why ~ Not today
Type One Human will always see this way
Ask if he is feeling well, pause, consider, sigh.
'Oh well, things may get better by and by.'
Look into the future you say, what do you see?
'Well I don't know, that's not really me.'
But it's a glorious day, shall we go for a ride?
'Oh there's the washing and ironing inside.'
This evening then, let's make a night to remember.
'I would but I have to save up now, for September.'
What are you saving for? You have everything you need.
'The roof may leak, the telly may break, the dogs to feed.'
Where shall we go on holiday, to the sun, by the sea?
'Oh no, I'd burn and get a rash, you know me.'
Well what then, do you just want to lay down and die?
'I'm sorry, I didn't mean it, honest, please don't cry.'
A night at home then, chips in front of the box for two.
'Not again, there's nothing on and it's all we ever do.'
Well I'm going out then, have a drink with friends.
'Go on then, leave me, that's how it always ends.'
I'm left to clean and work and sweat on my own at home,
While you go out enjoying yourself having fun alone.'
Close the door quietly in a controlled rage and go out
Feel guilty all night, exhausted by the mental boxing bout.

Irene Roberts

The Harbingers

Beyond the orbit of Pluto
Brought to Perihelion
By planetary perturbations;
The most brilliant appear
In the night sky above the sun.
The combined movement of the earth
Stand still against the star
Background, simply drifting away,
Heading directly towards the earth,
Their orbit take them right
Into the earth's twilight zone
Too faint to be seen.

M Cooper

Un-Found Love

Your thoughts are yours
My thoughts are mine
The gracious word, the Love
I have yet to define

Go on living
And keep on chasing
Through happiness and sorrow
The word Love so amazing

Love for you and when
I'm still so shy
Was it yesterday or tomorrow?
Will it stay with hello and after goodbye?

Love for some so easy
For others is so hard
Some are still seeking
Until from lips is barred

I wonder and wonder
For the Love deep down under
Is Love open for inspection?
Does it come from goodness and deception?

Friends are then friends
If the feeling is there
Now you are closer to Love
When everything you equally share

My poem is seeking *you*
Like seeking Love on and on
Hope to meet you one day
If not now ~ perhaps beyond

Philip Ellison

First Poem About Anything

What is all this talk of age.
It only means we have turned a page
Of life, which is meant to be lived
As happily as we know how,
Old age comes to everyone
Remember, age will happen to you
Soon, it will be your turn too.
The years disappear so quickly and fast
Nothing is ever made to last,
Enjoy each day, as it comes along.
Have a kindly word for the aged on song,
They have a store of knowledge to be told,
So listen to their tales of old
They may surprise you with their knowledge
Though they did not go to College.

K Glover

Computers For The Over 60's

I've just bought a computer and plugged it in today
To greet the new millennium a must for work and play
The screen is filled with colour much to my surprise
But what the hell is DOS or Windows 95
Up in the left hand corner is a thing they call a File
It said Save as HTML but it's hardly worth your while

The keyboard looked attractive, one key must do the trick
I typed in H-E-L and P and the words came back 'you're thick'
Hanging from the outside is a thing they call a mouse
It took the cat by surprise but he chased it round the house
The main thing is 'Don't panic' it's only a machine
So I cast my mind back forty years and the typists I had seen

I pressed F4 and then F9 and Caps Lock just for fun
What the hell's an Icon, I will have to ask my son
A one-hour phone call later told me all I had to know
A:/ or C/; to write to one you know
The computer answered quickly and the words came on the screen
Type in 'HELP', press 'RETURN' and print out what you've seen

I tried the FILE and EDIT, FORMAT, STYLE and then TOOLS
MACROS and then SMARTICONS underlined for fools
INSERT and then TOOLBARS they just spun round in my head
Then came the pretty pictures as I surfed around the WEB
WORD PERFECT seemed the answer as I tried to type my name
COMIC SANS or ROMAN TYPE they all appeared the same

This wasn't getting easier 'cos the MOUSE had nailed the cat
I couldn't change the little FONTS to see what I was at
At last I've found the PRINTER to print what I had done
One hundred copies later when all I want is one
They're bound to come in handy ~ I could hang them round my flat
Some MILESTONES showing flowers and things
And a picture of my cat

   Jonis Pastit

War Of Want

Have you ever known an MP,
Who had a road put through his house.
Or an MP on a waiting list,
To have his gall stones out.
I want free holidays, funny loans,
The power to bend the figures when I want to buy a home.
I want to be an anarchist, I want to right the wrongs,
I want to wave a flag and sing a marching song.
I want to cancel the licenses for the over 75's,
Then buy a bit of carpet for one of fat boy's dives.
I want to burgle junket joe
And check the police response time,
As if I didn't know.
I want to put a ferret up the weasel's trousers,
I want to hear him squawk
And I want to hear his language
In that funny plummy talk.

How could we know when we said yes,
That these extremely awful people,
Would make this extremely awful mess.

Doug Smith

The Last Electric Scarecrow

In every field in every land
an electric Scarecrow used to stand
piles of rag powered by high current
proffered the perfect deterrent
to prowling tigers and other predators
who burnt with birds, rodents, even alligators
and anything that touched the sacred pole
Then one day a Scarecrow found a soul
Transmigrated from a vagrant it killed
Just as the deity willed.
And when electric scarecrows were deemed obsolete
the money savers it did defeat.
Power was cancelled.
The Scarecrow danced,
tapping energy from the almighty sun,
storing it for nocturnal fun.
Animals fried.
People died.
The Scarecrow's home is now a cemetery
for tourists like us to see,
Provided we stay behind the gate
or death will also be our fate.

Paul Williams

Night Magic

I met a mystery woman
Beside the whispering sea,
We tarried together for a while
And let our souls run free,
                run free,
And let our souls run free.

I strolled with a mystery woman
Across the shadowed sands,
Her voice crooned soft upon the wind
And the waves spun white garlands,
                garlands,
And the waves spun white garlands.

I danced with a mystery woman
Saw the moon spark in her hair,
While the liquid languor of her eyes
Held secrets she could not share,
                not share,
Held secrets she could not share.

I left a mystery woman
As dawn-daggers scoured the night,
For it was the bitter, immutable hour
When dreams are put to flight,
                to flight,
When dreams are put to flight.

    John Rackham

Færie Found

Færie is back there:
    in the serene yards
    within the morning mist,
It is not the quiet porches
    or the nymph on the bird bath;
It is not within the trees
    or in the grass.

Færie is back there:
    in between the moments
    in the instant of no time and . . .
        no place;
It is the ethereal magic
    and the gossamer moment;
It is in the hearts and the minds
    and the soul's love for verdant Gæia.

John A Mills

How

How do trees grow mum?
How do we get the sky?
How do clouds appear?
And how do people cry?

How does the moon come out at night?
How come people die?
How come I have a fright at night?
How come dad bought me a kite?

How did we get names?
And how do you sink?
How do aliens come to earth?
And how did they make the colour pink?

How come we have cars?
How many friends have you?
How do you get on to a football team?
Please tell me how?

Callum Donnelly (9)

Blessing

May the wind bring you butterflies
The turning of days, sunflowers
The oceans, rivers of joy
The bells, peels of laughter
May sadness teach you about joy
May music teach you about stillness
May stillness teach you about God

Marianne Harvey

Love's Trials

Forty notes resounded to the sun
but the shy young girl heard only one
Seven times seven may be forty-three
but I love you and you love me
Little twists and bigger shapes
we calculate the lot
We often get it wrong
and I've just tied a knot
Small rooms, long wires, black clouds and little sun
you may even think there's nothing to be done
draw your holster tight, you may need your gun.

So the quack prescribes something from his nest
may God not have mercy, I need say nothing else
Jets and planes make trails through the sky
Shane picks an orange, let it all go by
Sleeping, eating, working for the boss
they really want to kill those who don't give a toss
Gamblers and drinkers, smokers and shades
lost souls on the bottle, dicing with the grave
Crazy paving, eerie noises, full moon, bad night
keep your wheelchair still, damn the men of might
Dark hour, then the dawn, you are guaranteed the light.

Patrick Fitzhenry

Spike

Her body's lithe. She's small white teeth and features sweet.
She glides across the room on silent dainty feet.
She's beautiful, intelligent, with bright and slanting eyes
and when she gets me into bed she will not let me rise
but cuddles up against my side, so soft and warm all night
and only shifts, reluctant, when I wake at morning light.
This lovely, soft, sleek beauty is only just thirteen
yet she treats me like an abject slave ~ I treat her like a queen.
You might think I'm a pervert, you'd be wrong in thinking that;
For my pretty, perfect, little queen's a tiny tabby cat.

D G W Garde

The Spectacle Brigade

We've been a Spectacle Brigade
For quite a long time now
We once were called a 'Young Wives Club'
But that was long ago.
We do not really call ourselves
By this new name you know
It's one that's just come to me
As more appropriate ~ so
If we complain that we can't read high posters
Or price tabs on Supermarket shelves
You'll know we're wearing them 'bifocals'
A warning not to get them for yourselves!
When young I could see for miles
Could thread my mother's needle in a twink
But now ~ my children ~ aware of all my trials
Come to my assistance ~ with a wink.

Greta E Bray

Love Of A Child

The love of a child, gentle fingers grasp your hand.
The stories you tell, their dreams of never, never land.
Words spoken in a jumble, only they will ever know.
The love in their hearts, this small child will show.

Tears that appear, in loving eyes that are blue.
They play you for the fool, but their ways are true.
They melt your heart, as they hold out their arms.
The heart of a parent, gives in, to their charms.

They harass you, bother you, till you give in.
They get excited, explaining where they have been.
They chatter forever, they could drive you wild.
But you are given, the love of your child.

They grow so quick, you wonder where the years have gone.
Was it only the other day, the birth of our son.
He brightens our day, he is funny through and through.
We treasure our angel, our love for him is true.

He is our baby boy, he is the one we prayed for.
He fills our life, has he been here before.
He is our son, even though he drives us wild.
We treasure the love, the love of our child.

Kevin P S Collins

Good Friends

The lion and the tiger went out to play
In the hot sunshine for their daily affray
Prodding each other in a warlike way
Hitting each other in a playful display

Said the tiger to the lion you are very hot
Perhaps you should stop hitting me such a lot
And come and join me on my little plot
And put up your feet and rest just a jot

Said the lion to the tiger you seem very kind
Maybe you should stop hitting me from behind
And let us see what both of us can find
And dine with each other till our stomachs are lined

Keith B Osborne

Sleep

Oh wondrous benison of sleep
That other world into which I creep
I drift and know I've found the place
Where warm, strong, gentle arms embrace
A haven of caring for which I've yearned
The joyfulness of love returned
Too soon comes dawn, the daylight see
And thrusts me back to reality.

Barbara Robson

Tea Time

A mouse crouched hiding behind a stone
From a cat that snooped close by.
He dare not move or hardly breathe,
Just glance through his tiny eye.

I'll find you soon, said the mean old cat.
You're not as smart as me.
You'll not escape my long sharp claws,
I'll eat you for my tea.

But very soon a dog rushed by
And the cat ran clean away.
Oh lucky mouse, you know you are,
You'll not be tea today.

Gerry Greaves

Venus Fly Trap

How is that love became litigation
to contest over possession,

How did we misplace love
on a mantle piece maybe,

One Pembroke table wholesale loss
love's safe deposit box,

How love's kiss my pearl
made me the oyster catcher,

Golden Oriole she unfurled
my top drawer no more,

Our signatures for paper officials
that fortune fold my heart,

Bankrupt then is my heart
love's property transferred,

Tears for the trustee
of whom this affair action bought,

At a price that my heart
has the sign to let,

One Venus fly trap
with judge and briefcase,

Bricklaying walls around our hearts
for a cottage industry,

Out there at the stockbroker's dance
Love was robbed by Falstaff.

Jeremy Jones

Broken Dreams

You have gone, and left me
Here all alone to mourn
For you and me,
What could have been,
Our dreams, our plans, cannot come true,
Now there is no longer you.
My eyes are dry I cannot cry,
Because, 'oh my dear', the
Pain is just too much to bear,
When I look around and you're not there,
Our broken dreams now, are in the past,
But memories of you will last and last.

Eileen P Dunn

The Patient Nurse

As I swap my tunic for a gown,
Upon my brow appears a frown,
Don't let this moment get you down!
All of life is but a stage
Each new thing at the turn of a page.
My tapestry is being woven
What is wrong, yet to be proven.
Amazing tests, today's technology,
Anxious I am, and I'll make no apology!
This is the place where they make diagnosis,
Medicines prescribed in so many doses.
Whatever the outcome, I'll live every day
With a vision of hope, even 'come what may'
For this I am sure, I will live 'till I die.
Then go to my new home, up in the sky!

    Chrissie McGrew

Love And Hate

Whispers and sighs,
Gentle as a summer breeze,
When love is in the air.

Harsh words and screams,
Discordant as a winter storm,
When hate is in the air.

Loving and hating,
Twin emotions inextricably
Entwined within us.

Feelings can change
Chameleon-like throughout our lives,
Coloured by circumstance.

Welcome sweet love,
The harbinger of happiness,
Spreading its warmth around.

Resist the urge
To nurture seeds of hate
That tear the soul apart.

Sunshine or storm,
Blue skies or frowning clouds,
The choice is solely ours.

Let love prevail,
Enriching every part of us ~
For hatred can destroy.

Roma Davies

To My Beloved Children

My Candle is beginning to flutter
The warning is clear in the air
I cannot sleep without thinking
Everything beginning to fit
The jigsaws of life,
Come nearer and nearer in sight
I'll soon know all the answers
But alas, unable to tell them to you
The passing spirits are touching
I feel no pain or fear
I must leave with no farewells
No kiss or cuddle to prove
How much I have truly loved you
I think I'll take a part of each of you
Leaving a part of me
If I arrive at that wonderful place
That we have been taught to believe
If your faith and memories remain long
I'll ask *him* to help you all
If troubles befall
I'll prepare a palace for you too
Your beds will be soft
Your days will be good
No pain, each day a joy
This wee letter is to you *all*.

    My beloved children.

    Winifred Parkinson

Come Closer

God where are You,
I need You here
I need Your help
I know You're close
As I feel Your presence.
Come closer,
Let me touch You, hold You
I will then know that I am safe.
Lord I want You to stay with me
To go wherever I go,
Come and teach me
Come and guide me,
Take this key to my life
Unlock the door and come in
As I want You here by my side for eternity.

Alison Fewins

A Visitor To The Harvest Festival

Our chapel were full to the doors on the night,
As full 'as a foot in a shoe',
When the harvest were held, as it were every year
After croppin' and pickin' were through.

All the fields were now empty, the stubble were burnt,
And the barns were full up with the hay;
The trees in the orchards stripped back to the bough,
As we gathered together to pray.

We all met together to thank the dear Lord
For the harvest we'd all gathered in;
And the chapel, done up like a maid for her beau
Looked a picture, just like a new pin.

O, the chapel were full to the doors on that night
With folks who 'ad come from around,
And when Pastor stood up in the pulpit and said:
'Let's all pray,' you could not hear a sound ~
Except for the clock that ticked on the wall
And the wind whistling under the door;
So we all bowed 'us 'eads, and some folk knelt down,
While children just sat on the floor.

And I tell 'e, the smell in the chapel that night
Were lovely, as lovely could be;
And the flowers displayed in the vases and jars
Were a picture for all there to see.

There were apples and carrots and 'ops 'anging down,
There were lettuce and cabbage and pears,
And a big sheaf of corn with a sash round its girth
Looking lovely, propped up by the stairs.

And at first, it seemed funny to me when I saw
A big lump of coal on the floor,
But then I remembered that, that bit o' coal
Was a bit o' creation, and more ~
For apart from the fruit and the veg and the nuts,
There were water and salt by the door.

We sang all the 'ymns that we usually sing
When harvest time comes round again,
Like 'Ploughin' the fields and 'scatt'rin' the seed'
And prayin' for 'life-givin' rain.'

O, I think it's so lovely, this time of the year
When life's 'ectic pace settles down,
And the people who gather in our little chapel
Come in from the country and town.

Well, that's how it were on this 'ticular night
What I've bin a-telling you of;
Seems that everyone there had a *'thank you'* to say
To the Lord of the harvest ~ to God.

And as we all sat on the pews and the chairs
To sing 'arvest 'ymns in God's 'ouse;
I noticed, just under the pulpit, there sat
A bright-eyed and brown 'arvest mouse!

Don Barker

A Special Gift!

To a very special *Daughter*
Who gave her brother . . .
A rather special Gift!
She fills our lives with laughter
At times . . . to give us a big lift,
Her brother became very ill
It really was a problem . . .
For which he could not take a pill,
He had to have *Dialysis* . . .
Which helped him for a while . . .
But he really needed a Kidney!
To give him back his smile,
So along came little *Sis:*
With the answer to the solution:
She offered to Donate a Kidney . . .
and was found to be a perfect match,
So they had the operation:
The *Kidney* was named *Sydney!*
By theatre and medical staff.
So a brother has his life back ~
and an extra lift!
Due to a very loving Sister . . .
And a daughter . . . who gave an
Extra special gift!

Anna Marie

Positive Thinking ~ On Winter

There are *two* ways of looking without a doubt
From the outside in, and the inside out
When you're out on the street feeling frozen stiff
You can warm yourself up again easily if
You wear a hat, a scarf and gloves
Buy a mug of soup and keep on the move.
Keep walking though the bus doesn't come
You might even end up walking home
To a lovely warm house, with the heating on,
A delicious hot meal of Dumplings and stew
Topped by sponge pud and Custard and steaming brew
Of Tea, or of Coffee, it just matters not
Then sit and watch Telly, or Slob out, or Read
Then run a Hot Bath and go off to Bed.

Emma Dronfield

Angel

If angels fly, why do you walk?
You do not speak, but your lips talk,
Your eyes of summer an' shivers with your touch,
So much to say, so much in love.

The days are long, but the nights are longer,
While the weak don't survive, the strong get stronger,
A moment's kiss is this unfound wish,
To hold you in my arms would be untold bliss.

I'd buy you a rose but it wouldn't survive,
Not like this love it will be with me until I die,
The waves are getting bigger as they swallow me up,
So much to say, so much in love.

You're the peach on the tree, the leaf floating in the sea,
You're everything that I want you to be.

Paul Ingham

Christmas Celebration

Children the world over always remember
the 25th of December.
Perhaps not for the right reasons, for most
children, it is the time for presents and toys.
When I was a girl it was a Christmas stocking
that was filled.
And for little items like pencils and crayons, a
scarf and a doll we were thrilled.
We were so easily pleased, a little then could
seem such a lot and really what sensible parents.
We are living in a different era, our children of
today would find this quite strange.
Now it's videos and video games from a very early age.
Nothing now seems to be moving at a steady pace, it
has almost become a race.

Lots of children even today don't and won't even realise
Christmas is the celebration of the birth of Christ.
They will have missed all the lovely stories of baby Jesus
lying in a manger, because there was no room in the inn.
And in a stable he was born away from the noise and din.
And the shepherds being visited by an angel proclaiming
the birth of a new king, and how 3 wise men journed far
being led by a shining star, to welcome him.
As a child I never tired of listening and reading about the
baby born to bring peace and hope in the world.
I remember being muffled up with a scarf, woolly hat and
mittens braving the cold weather to sing carols.
This yearly Christmas treat was greeted with pleasure.
Christmas is a time of happiness and goodwill, when families
and friends unite in love, to celebrate a very special birthday.

Elizabeth Myra Crellin

The Gift Of Time

I heard a thousand blended notes
As I sat on that incline,
I heard a thousand blended notes
Not one of them was mine.

Of this I would not disseminate
E'en breath seems to incriminate.
Below me, before me, was paradise sublime
And yet, and true, that none of this was mine.

Mesmeric pool, and reeds erect
No atmospheric disturbance yet,
This picture of tranquillity, Oh no! Not mine
But orderliness, yes, ordered for all time.

The matching of nature, so very fine
Fitting for a canvas where I am sitting,
Or a painting, nothing foreign to the setting,
To Let for one short space of time,

And yet enduring to the changing face
Of seasons coming on apace.
Now, the shades of night remorselessly encroaching
The curtain of the night descending.

The blended notes of bird song disappear
Blended only in the senses
For memories to administer to tortured souls
Some way ahead when there is time.

There are these places yet to find
For tortured souls from daily grind,
For minds still fettered; searching avidly,
If man alone, would let it be.

   Fred Simpson

The Magic Of A Home

We drove through a driveway of wonderful greenery,
A truly magical hand had set this scenery.
The façade of the house was large and beautiful,
Just the view alone, would have kept it full.
Stately, black and white like an olde world inn,
It's welcome and tranquillity shining from within.
The day was hot, the Sun all one could desire,
Shone through reflected windows, like balls of fire.
All rooms were furnished in white and gold,
What historic tales those walls could have told.
Flowers grew in profusion at the front of the house,
While vast sleepy meadows, had young rabbits running about.
Long velvet lawns stretched out here and there,
Sown by a knowing hand with loving care.
Lots of loving thought went into a house such as this,
Where else but in England, could you find such bliss!?

Margaret Hubball

Green

Earth is fit to be seen,
In the loveliest colour vivid green.
So what does it mean,
Read the lines for ~ between.
Countryside lawn, wherever you go,
Green predominates the world and vegetables grow.
Cabbages, spring onions, marrows for us to eat,
All on our land, and all at our feet.

Maria Carmen Lee Costello

In Memoriam di Leandro Tintinalli 1910-2000
(Dedicated to my most dear grandfather who died on 29.12.2000)

Fort William was never the same, when they gave Leandro his name.
With the heart of the truest family man, and born unto us,
    Across oceans, clouds, and beneath yonder stars,
The soul of his strength was always so proud,
    And his love was our family; his world was our crowd.
Stoking the tender, and mining for gold,
    His graft was of hardship, his courage always so bold.
And he built his house in Red Lake, for his family with spouse,
    Never leaving their pockets to empty or go without food.
He was always a friend, to his friends, to the world,
    Always a husband to Yolanda his wife,
And a father to Franco, Velma, and Rita to whom he gave a life.
    His love was enduring his smile forever did shine,
As a grandfather in Windsor, he became greater than any in time.
    And now in his passing may God keep his memory and soul,
So we pass on his story throughout our lives year after year.

Anthony Rosato

North West

By Elk lake in north west Canada in a log cabin sheltered by a
belt of pine lived a Sarcee Indian known as Moccasin Pete
All should have been well but he sat in a chair nursing a glass
that held two fingers of whiskey neat
Which would not do at all as drunkenness would lose him his
livelihood as guide to hunting parties
His customers were executive city men who paid well for his
service and expected to find him hale and hardy
It was of paramount importance that he sober up for his sake
He knew that a pontoon plane was already on its way to the lake
With a shudder he tried hard not to think about the fire
But the mental picture of their former cabin home kept coming
back to him that had accidentally become his wife's pyre
He missed her feminine company
and their happy marriage that had spanned many years
Some hours later the expected aircraft's nearing drone caught
his ears
Sober now washed and shaved he quickly put a clean shirt on and
shut the cabin door behind him and ran down to the shore
Aboard the plane he knew there would be a pre-booked party of four
The float plane circled overhead then came down to meet the lake
in a watery glide
He rowed toward the bobbing aircraft soon he was listening to the
men who had been on the plane telling him how they envied him
living in such beautiful surroundings and
how lucky he was to be a hunting
guide.

   D T Fletcher

Squishy And Icky

Squishy was a squashy slug,
Who lived beneath a carpet rug,
That had been thrown out in the shed,
And served as cover for his head.

His only friend was Icky Bug,
Who lived upon a carpet rug,
That had been thrown out with the junk,
And made for him a comfy bunk.

One day they thought they should explore,
The world outside the old shed door,
So off they went, excitement growing,
Passing fields with great beasts lowing.

Then they stopped to have some tea,
With what appeared a friendly bee,
But they not knowing anything,
Weren't prepared for a nasty sting.

Home they went and said 'No more!
We'll never venture through that door,
The world outside is not for us,
It's caused us too much stress and fuss!'

'It's warm and cosy in the shed,
It serves as cover overhead,
We've got a warm and comfy bed,
There's lots of food to keep us fed.
If we go outside, we'll end up dead,'
Said Squishy. And Icky agreed, 'Well said.'

Mo Bailey

SOS

Has anyone here seen our Grandma?
She's cuddly and terribly old.
Her hair has gone wispy, her teeth have dropped out,
and she never does what she is told.

She went off to market quite early one day
for veg; and a nice piece of steak,
and said she'd meet up with Matilda, her friend,
for a chat over coffee and cake.

She hasn't come home and it's pouring with rain.
Matilda says Grandma had said,
'There's a new place that's opened up, just down the road.
We'll go to that Cafe instead.'

Last seen going in for a nice cup of tea
to the *Internet Cafe* in town,
she flew into Cyber Space, Surfing the Net,
and doesn't know how to get down.

So put into action the Search Key and Mouse,
with Floppy Disc, CD and Rom,
or make up a Spreadsheet and Open a Site
for World Wide Web Grandma dot com.

We want her back here in her chair by the fire,
not Virtual, but Real, with her treats
and tales of her childhood, so press all the keys;
but *hands off* the one that Deletes.

She says things were different when she was a child.
She understands knitting and such,
but can't do computers or video games.
We want her back so very much.

Has anyone here seen our Grandma?
She's cuddly and terribly old.
Her hair has gone wispy, her teeth have dropped out
and she shouldn't stay out in the cold.

Barbara Young

Progress?

This is progress; is this how it's done?
Robbed of her glory; stripped to the bone;
The lady Britannia bending her knee
And weeping in shame for all to see.
Old enemies smile; no mercy there.
Hands reach out ~ they want a share.
Piece by piece the motherland sold,
No pride left in the lust for gold.
Stripping assets; cutting the cost;
The race is on to acquire the most.
The green fields vanish; the quiet ways
Are lost in an acrid, fume-laden haze.
The rich grow richer while the poor despair ~
Does anyone see? Does anyone care?
Our heritage doomed by the stroke of a pen,
While tomorrow it starts all over again.

Vivian Finlay

A Cry For Help

The spiders spin their webs of deceit
With the ants ordering their Soldiers to meet
The killer bees that can strike at will
And the bloodthirsty lion that likes his fill,
This world of ours can be so alarming
With blood and gore that's never charming
We tend to forget the poor and needy
With a child crying out '*Mum* please feed me.'
We think of ourselves and what we can gain
And never remember the people in pain
To change our world would take time to come
But Hey! There is always the next Millennium.

William D Watt

I'm Bored!

Children coming home from school,
Mummy, Daddy, we hear them call.
Please can you tell us what we can do?
Here's a few things for the both of you.
Watch TV, draw, or write,
Look for the 'Man in the Moon' at night.
Tweenies, Rugrats or Art Attack,
Look up at the ceiling
    Lying on your back.
These are a few things for you to do,
Or we can just cuddle right up to you.

    Darron Furness

Bats In The Attic

I strolled in the moonlight
And looked at the sky.
I saw a dark shape
And a bat glided by.
There are bats in my attic
And I'm really ecstatic
Though I only watch from the ground.
They never wear ties
But they gobble up flies
And I'm happy to know they're around.

I hope they feel welcome,
I'd like them to stay.
I don't want to frighten
Or chase them away.
There are bats in my attic
And I'm really ecstatic
Though I only watch from the ground.
They can't prune a rose
But they hang by their toes
And I'm happy to know they're around.

Bats often sleep up in
Church towers by day,
In caves or tree-trunks
But I'm happy to say
There are bats in my attic
And I'm really ecstatic
Though I only watch from the ground.
They can't count to six,
But they eat up the tics.
They can't bake a pie,
But they really can fly!
They can't roller-skate,
But I still think they're great,
And I'm happy to know they're around!

Jill Darby

Tide

The tide is always ebb or flowing, where's it been, where's it going?
It never stays long in one spot, now it's in, now it's not!
The tide is either in or out, it never seems to hang about,
Always going to where it's been, on staying here it's not too keen.
When tide is high, then it follows, that in other parts there must be hollows,
Well the same amount of sea is shared, some is here and some is there,
The moon is blamed for all this motion, that lifts the seven seas and oceans,
But does the answer lie in space; could it be us, the human race?

Imagine, that each summer long, people on to beaches throng,
And everyone just can't resist, the urge to throw, you just can't miss!
Young boys, some big, some tiny, all throw stones into the briny,
And every throw makes ripply action, which could set off a chain reaction!
All round the globe, in each resort, are little ripples joining force,
They gain momentum and soon after, big waves are formed, now which tale's dafter?
The moon is just a great big face that lovers need for their embrace
That poets need to rhyme with June, what makes the tides? Can't be the moon!
It's young boys; it stands to reason, they throw their stones each summer season,
In spring our tides are worse, no wonder, Aussie boys now throw stones down-under!

Michael Cooper

All Children ~ Beware

On Halloween Night,
At the end of the day,
The Halloween Folk
Come out to play.
Mischief makers,
Witches' Brew,
You'd better be careful ~
They're after you.
Small piggy eyes,
They're short and squat,
With big hooked noses
And teeth full of rot.
They'll grab you
And pinch you,
And pull at your hair ~
Scream out loud
They won't even care.
So take my advice,
And stay safe inside,
And if you hear knocking,
Run quickly and hide!

Louise Stokes

God Is With Us

God is with us
In our hearing and listening
Laughing and crying
In our coming and going
Night and day.

God is with us
In the morning when we awake
He took care of us whilst we slept
He is with us while we were at school
In our rest and play.

God is with us
He helps us in our daily tasks
But when worries come
If help we need, we need only ask
He is with us through our sadness,
Sorrows, troubles and joy.

God is with us
He helps us through our daily lives
We thank you Lord for all that you do
For your loving care
And knowing that you are always there.

S Peters

A Cake Of Peace

Carefully fold together, a portion of Jealousy, Greed, Lust and Hate,
When mixed, beat until frothy, discard, then prepare to change your fate.
Now, take a large portion of Love and blend well with a large dollop of Happiness,
Add just a sprinkling of Zest, and colour with Joyfulness.
Now cook the whole thing with the warm glow of Pacification
And Tranquillity, Serve, then stand back and watch true relaxation.

Let all the Nations of the world unite and taste
The true flavour of a Peace not brought about in haste,
Let all the peoples relax and sing the praises of the brave,
Who dare to make the cake of peace, and who by so doing save
The population from the gluttony of war and carnage,
Defending the world from any more danger and damage.

This is the recipe for Joy and Peace,
Try the cake and let all wars cease.

Francis Allan Hoggarth

The Book Of Love

Open up the book of love and you will see before your eyes
A story to keep in your heart
Written to help make us more enlightened and wise

Page one tells us always be kind, helpful and good
Above these words is the picture of a peaceful snow-white dove

Page two is based on sharing, caring and never showing greed
Don't have a selfish heart, then a better life you will lead

Page three says never hurt your friends
Or be cruel to animals and mankind
Follow these rules throughout your life and love you will find

Page four asks us to nurse the sick and elderly
Show everyone you care
And remember God gave the world for us all to share

Page five brings stories of laughter, merriment and mirth
We all want happy smiley faces spread around the earth

Page six pleads don't argue with friends, never shout out loud
Don't let a loving friendship suffer under a stormy black cloud

Page seven looks at nature and the beauty of the countryside
Help preserve this precious land, and sea with turning tide

Page eight, befriend the lonely in their hour of need
Take them by the hand and into a better life lead

Page nine, let's unite regardless of creed and race
Have fun together no matter the colour of your face

Page ten tells us the secret, where to find this book
These words are written on your heart
Read them carefully and you will find good luck.

Maxine Kaye

Sad And Blue

When you're feeling sad and blue
Think of an angel
She'll be watching over you
An angel dances
An angel sings
An angel wears her golden ring
Angelic with a glow
She's there to guide us
And forever be beside us
When you're thinking of doubts and fears
An angel comes and takes your tears
When the sadness is lifted above
An angel comes and sends her love
When the blues drift into space
An angel comes and takes its place

Gibby

A Question Of Dying

Do people die when they get old?
I asked my Uncle Ted.
Could they be walking down the road
And you'd see them drop down dead?

How old is old? I need to know.
Great Grandma's ninety-eight.
My Grandma's only fifty so
She's got a while to wait.

Do people know they're going to die?
Do they get a poorly head?
If I knew I was going to die
I'd snuggle down in bed.

Does dying feel like going to sleep?
Or do you hurt inside?
Or do you go all dizzy,
Like a roller coaster ride?

Does going to Heaven feel quite nice,
Like floating through the air?
Is God expecting you to come?
Will He be waiting there?

And when you're dead, d'you know you're dead?
Do you think that you might find
You miss your friends on earth too much?
Are you allowed to change your mind?

Diana S L Cook

The Mouse

Why do the ladies scream and shout
Because they've seen me dart about?
Why do the men put down a trap
That closes with a fearful snap?
I'm just a small and friendly mouse
Who'd like to live inside your house.

I promise I'll be very good
And only nibble at your food.
All day I'll stay inside my nest
Until at night in bed you rest.
Upstairs and down I'll then explore
And leave my droppings on your floor.

And when a family comes along
You'll love to hear their squeaky song.
The holes they'll chew for you at night
I'm sure will fill you with delight!
And sometimes, for a special treat,
May we have some cheese to eat?

And some bacon and some bread?
For hungry babies must be fed!
Please let me have a habitat,
Safe from owl and stalking cat,
A tiny space within your home,
For a friendly mouse of your very own!

J O Coatswith

The Trees Speak

The trees
in the park
talk to each other.
Whenever there's a breeze
they whisper softly together,
or murmur, as if they're worried.
On windy days you can hear them roaring.
Are they quarrelling among themselves,
or are they angry with us people, for
chopping them down?
On still
days
they
just
stand
quietly.

Julia Davenport

The Greedy Bunny

Woodland creatures come to see,
Bessie snooze beneath a tree,
It's Easter morning, bright and sunny,
And that naughty little Bunny,
Chocolate wrappers at her feet,
She's eaten up her Easter treat,
Every single little crumb,
Safely tucked inside her tum,
She must know she ought to share,
But perhaps she doesn't care,
Being greedy isn't funny,
What a selfish little Bunny.

J E Lovell

A Highland Morning

The day 'tis bleak with Highland mist,
The burns run cold through the heathered valleys,
Wind howls wildly o'er the immense steep hills,
And the flowers shrink from the icy gale.
A river gushes through a murky woodland,
And the salmon leap over the swirling falls.
I sit and watch from a small rocky outcrop,
Transfixed by the surging, beautiful canal,
The bitter cold bites my blood,
As the grey clouds saunter in overhead,
A beautiful morn in a Highland mist.

Sally Bosson

The Queen Mother

Stayed to face the bombs
Could relate to East Enders
Visits scars of war.

Elegant lifestyle
Restored the Royal image
Centenarian.

She's two Queen Mothers
One, private woman in tweeds
Gumboots and Corgi's.

Eileen Pearce

You Know Who You Are!

If we had peace there would be more laughter
More Joy in the world, more fun,
And just for once don't you think we deserve it
You've had your day ~ when all said and done.

If we had peace there would be more kindness
More giving of self, more truth,
Our children would go back to being children
And understanding between parent and youth.

If we had peace there would be a mildness
Of spirit and behaviour and tongue,
Think twice before a word or an action
Think again for fear of doing it wrong.

If we had peace we would have self-control
A not wanting to do anyone any harm
Whatever our life may consist of
Everyone needs to feel safe and warm.

If we had peace we would need long-suffering
A quality to work on every day,
Because we're not perfect we will get upset
Perhaps now we could learn how to pray.

If we had peace there would be a goodness
That comes from these qualities above,
Every decent thought would be carried along
By genuine acts and feelings of love.

And so if we learned how to pray once again
Do you think we might gain a semblance of faith?
I know that it's possible ~ it will be achieved
If not for self then for families sake.

Susie J Burnette

History Repeats

The devastation of a land
Cloaked in the wounds
That can never heal.

The helplessness of a mother
Waving her little soldier off to war ~
Will she ever see him again?

Wars waged by mankind upon mankind
Since the beginning of time.
History repeats itself again, and again, and again.

There is a lesson here,
If we could only see
Through our blind stupidity.

 Gail Lawson

Enemy Awareness

Our sky once reddened with Galactic mist
are now reddened by our Scientist.
As our earth prepares for war
with nuclear defences our atmosphere's poor.
Once nature's elements were calm and placid
now our rain is full of acid.
Rumbles in the sky, from a great height
not clouds, but aircrafts at the speed of light.
Once white surf covered our sea lands
now grey foam rolls over our sands.
Our food crops now grow slow and poor
that natural healthy glow, exist no more.
Our natural resources are now so crude
they put additives in our food.
Our wildlife habitat's disappearing at haste
as likely due to nuclear waste.
Our fresh clean air, once a worldwide topic
now filled with destruction that's microscopic.
Powerful inventions meant to defend
are bringing our earth to a fatal end.
So when our hair falls to the floor
just ask yourself, who won the war.
To healthy people this poem I dedicate
for if our skin starts blistering, it's probably too late.

L Iles

Turkish Disaster Appeal

Buildings in villages came crashing to the ground,
Mass devastation, visible for miles around:
Families wiped out, too many to mention,
Survivors in need of care and attention.

Rescuers worked throughout day and night,
Searching through debris, immune to their plight;
Hoping more assistance will soon arrive,
As they recovered a child, they have found alive.

Further tremors could strike the region,
But medics strive on, like the Roman Legion;
Blood transfusions, help put patients at ease,
Whilst Cholera and Typhoid are causing disease.

People are filled with sadness and sorrow,
Not knowing what will happen tomorrow;
Medical resources are desperately needed,
So the sick and the injured, will not be impeded.

Water supplies are perilously low,
Food distribution is desperately slow;
Living in tents under the midday sky,
As the temperatures reach extremities high.

The world is united with helping hands,
For people suffering, in foreign lands;
A small donation will help aid relief,
To those refugees, who are stricken with grief.

M Goat

Children Of The World

In this world of ours
Turmoil stands at its head,
Countries fight with one another
Where peace should reign instead,
The children of the world are the future for us all
But some hungry power people don't seem to care at all,
What example do our children see
Of morals, justice and honour,
What chance do we stand the parents of this future
When we try to teach our children right from wrong,
You countries of the world
Remember to your shame,
Don't let the few who see power and gain
As all that matters
Bring goodness to its knees in tatters,
For when they are all long gone
It's our children of the world and their
Future that matters.

Mary Neill

The Cave

Buried in my memory
is a place I seldom go
for fear of disturbing strangers
I tread the path I know.

But sometimes when I'm brave
I step off the beaten track
and shout into a cave
which throws my question back.

Listening to the echo
my voice resounding off the wall
I recall an empty shadow
whose silence said it all.

Stephanie Munro

Blue Guitar

The guitar stands neglected in the corner.
It has no outstanding features,
other than a missing second string.
It does not belong to Carlos Santana or
Eric Clapton or Jeff Beck or Gary Moore.
It does not have a distinctive sound,
like Hank Marvin's Fender Stratocaster.
Nor a name like B B King's 'Lucille'.

It's just a guitar that's done nothing of note,
languishing alone in an upstairs room.
It no longer strums chords with the Beatles,
nor picks out a blues to the Stones.
It doesn't twang tunes with the Shadows,
or rasp boldly in time to the Kinks.
It just lies on its own, dejected,
straining to hear some distant CD.
Yearning for fingers, to touch those strings.

Paul Kelly

What Is It?

It's with us every day,
Yet it can't be seen.
All living things rely on it,
Without it, there would be nothing.

We cry out for it,
From the moment of birth.
It's the one thing needed,
By all, on this earth.

From a blade of grass,
To that old, old tree.
From a bird flying high,
To a fish in the sea.

From nature's first,
To nature's last.
Without it, all would be in the past.
Nothing on this earth would last.

What is it?
Of course, it's the air we breathe.
It fills the whole wide world.
It's a free gift to us all!

Anita Bricknell

Alfriston Scene

The snow is banked high and crisp
    and the cool winter sun casts faint shadows
The remaining autumn leaves hang feathery
    and tufts of grass protrude in meadows
The church roof and steeple are white with frost
    and the tops of walls are snowy iced
The ivy twisting round the trees is lacy now
    firm holly berries scarlet shine, their seedlings spiced
The sheep are driven home from hollow ground
    up the hill to the safety of their fold
The shepherd is hungry for his home
    his body wrapped against the cold
The downs are white and roundly stark
    their ancient mounds seem coldly bare
The Roman and the Saxon paths
    lead to where their kin were buried there
One cannot escape the force of time
    its pull upon our ancestral bequest
Of the English soil this English place
    to leave it as such, is our subsequent test.

G Carpenter

The Dome (We Actually Went There)

Yesterday we went to the Dome,
Just twelve hours later and we were back home,
Two hours or so in a coach each way
And at the Dome for the rest of the day.

'What did you think of it?' people all ask
And land you with the impossible task
Of explaining why your hair was not curled
By seeing the biggest tent in the World.

The building's impressive, the Arena so great,
That it swallows up thousands, who patiently wait
For the show that occurs just twice every day.
('Twice is enough' is all I'll say!)

The main things to see are queues and more queues,
Which seem to take much more time than the views.
We didn't see much, because most of the time
We spent on the outside, because it was fine!

    P Davies

Nemesis

He'd exceeded the escape velocity
And floated off into space:
    Was it levity or depravity
    To defy the force of gravity
    And breach the cosmic cavity
Where only stars have a place?

His speed increased exponentially
Till it approached the velocity of light:
    He felt he was nearing divinity,
    But at 10 million miles a minute he
    Shot off towards infinity,
Which served him darn well right!

A M Woolman

All Of Me . . .

Today I am on a new hospital wing
I'm feeling quite good, I could even sing
I feel safe and secure, with the hospital staff
In fact quite often they make me laugh

In stating the obvious, on this mental health ward
When in trouble, you can just pull a cord
People around you, loneliness aborted
Let's hope, while I'm here, my life's troubles will be sorted

To stop depression, to most seems simple
Make us happy and laugh, 'til we show a dimple
'Cos, happiness, is one step to recovery
The doc and his staff, have made this discovery

There seems no end to my bodily malfunction
I wish all my doctors, would meet at some junction
Because I have a separate doctor, for each different part of me
But . . . I only have one, whole person, one body, for anyone to see

So I implore, please pull together
'Cos I'm going down, in life's stormy weather
I'm drowning in this medical maze
That's why now, my mind's in a constant haze.

Operations I have had in abundance, to date
But it's my brain condition, that will seal my fate
So I hope, on this new hospital wing
That it will eventually, good health bring . . .

   Janice Walpole

Broken Trust

How can I forgive you when I don't know what to say?
How can I live with you when my heart has lost its way?
How can I ever tell you that my life was torn apart
The day you said you couldn't be with me. You broke my heart.

I loved you with a passion that was so intense, so rare
I didn't think there'd ever be a day when you weren't there
But blinded by my feelings of ignorance and youth
I failed to see so clearly the horrid, painful truth

That I was just a habit that forms itself with time
And every time I see you I'm reminded of your crime
You let me think you loved me before you gave confession
The die was cast, the damage done, I'd formed the wrong impression

With such a simple sentence you destroyed my perfect dream
But I've learnt a sorry lesson, things aren't always what they seem
I'll take more care in future to avoid the tears, the pain
But I know it will take time before I give my heart again

Anne Wheble

A Wild Night

The wind whistles fiercely over the moor.
Howling with fury, as it tries to enter the door.
The letter box lifting and banging, the dog in a frenzy
barking, barking, 'tis only the wind I tell her, she still
runs to see.
As the wind blows harder, flattening the heather,
signalling a prelude to a great storm, we should have
heeded the weatherman, for he did warn, come let us
batten the hatches, and find the matches, for we'll soon
be in the dark you and me.
Now lass, if there's to be lightning, it will be but a
spark, and if there is thunder too,
hide under the table, just as I used to do.
I will look after you lass, don't worry,
Oh why is this wind in such a hurry!

A loud crash is heard from outside amid the din.
That will be the old tree down at last, I thought it
would go, its boughs so thin.
That is more sawing and chopping for me tomorrow,
I wonder how all the animals are fairing, thankfully the
small ones will be safe in their burrow.

Come to me lass, it won't last much longer,
I cannot believe the wind can grow any stronger.
A sudden flash, darkness everywhere, matches and candles
in a heap.
The good dog beneath the table, as I fall over a chair,
cursing and swearing, I take a great leap.
What a wild night, as several hours later the storm
abates, come to me lass, rest your head,
the letter box is still now, 'tis time for you and I, to
get to our bed.

Helen Phillips

Boys . . .

If I could do just what I liked I'd do away with boys
I'd un-invent them, send them off and fill my time with toys.
They're cheeky, loud, they're rude and brash to name only a new
They sniff a lot, have dirty knees, and pick their noses too.
The boys in our class always smell, their hair is full of fluff
They cheat at sums, are always late, their shirts have dirty cuffs.
In dancing class they stand around and sulk like lumps of lard
The teachers say 'Just pick a girl, it cannot be that hard!'
If you're unlucky, Billy Clegg will squeeze you half to death,
Tread on your toes with puffs and blows and gas you with his breath.
At Christmas when we're in our play, around the crib we'll lean
The silly boys will make a noise and try to steal the scene.
If good at sums they're ugly, if good at sport
they're thick
And whenever we play hockey I just hit them with my stick.
Is there not a place to send them? Could we tie them to a tree?
For if the world was full of girls no better place there'd be.

Elaine Spence

Harvest

Harvest's about sharing
for those very poor
Harvest's about helping
so people have more

Farmers share crops
and give them away
If you can help us
you would make someone's day

Bread, biscuits, fruit and more
to please somebody at their door

So bring something in
it could be cold or hot
They would be very grateful
you would please them such a lot

Jemma Towler

New Babies

My mum is singing softly to the baby on her knee
I really can't remember if she softly sang to me
This new baby makes a lot of noise for such a little thing
Maybe when she's as big as me she will learn to sing

The baby's gone to sleep at last, so peaceful in her cot
Now she isn't crying, I love her quite a lot
Mum holds out her arms to me, I climb upon her knee
As she gently holds me, she softly sings to me

My mum is singing softly to the baby on her knee
As I watch them I recall how she softly sang to me
When the baby's fast asleep, then her job is done
I look upon the peaceful face that is my new-born son

Christine Edwards

Bats

What creature is more noble
than the Greater horseshoe bat ~
and surely bats are preferable
to cat or rat or gnat?
A bat may be a Natterer
or parti-coloured ~ fun!
Or like the Greater mouse-eared bat
inclined to be more glum!

They may not have good eyesight,
but their hearing is acute ~
though most bats prefer insects ~
the fruit bat may like fruit.
It's surely a mistake to think
that bats may be unhealthy ~
and really bats grow tired of that
old pun, bats in a belfry!

Or clever, witty sayings like:
'You're blind as any bat!'
Their ultra-sonic signals show
they know much more than that!
And when folks say: 'You're batty!'
They just show their ignorance ~
before the 1900's
people had a lot more sense!

Kenneth Berry

To You Dear Mother

A message to my mother,
Wherever you may be,
Alone at home, with company, or me,
I will always love you,
At night or in the day,
Love will always be with you,
And there is where it'll stay.

Kirsten Cassidy

The Alphabet

A is for apples found on a tree
B is for baking them for tea
C is for cupboard, cup and cat
D is for dog that sits on the mat
E is for eggs on the kitchen shelf
F is for flower I can pick myself
G is for ground, gravel and grass
H is for houses we often pass
I is for Ian, iron and inn
J is for jumping, jelly and Jim
K is for kite blowing away
L is for learning we do each day
M is for money, monkey and might
N is for nurses, noisy and night
O is for orange, a fruity drink
P is for puzzles that make you think
Q is for quiver, quaver and quite
R is for robin, his breast's so bright
S is for sunshine, shiver and shoes
T is for two, the terrible twos
U is for ugly, useless and under
V is for vanity, vintage and Vander
W is for walking, worker and wet
X is for X-ray done by the vet
Y is for year, yesterday and you
Z is for Zara, zebra and zoo

Lillian Jones

Little Angels Nursery

There's trouble in our nursery
'Cause little Johnny's had a wee
In the sandpit, he's so cool.
He got told off by Mrs Poole!

Then naughty Paul, him over there,
Put playdough in Samantha's hair.
When they tried to get it out
You should have heard her scream and shout!

The Lego's flushing down the loo,
Tom did that and I did too,
But not quite all, it's good you see,
I'm gonna take some home with me!

Then we found a huge great spider,
Thought it would be fun to hide her
In that lovely biscuit tin.
I wish someone would bring it in!

Lorna's done some coloured balls
On the paper on the walls,
And Amy's cutting teddy bears
In the curtains by the chairs!

Oh no, I can see my dad.
Most days I'd be very glad,
But we've had so much fun today
I think I'd really like to stay!

Julia Donaldson

Apple Tree

O apple tree, O apple tree,
Why is the fruit you bare,
So bright and fruity, crisp and juicy,
Surrounding me everywhere?

O apple tree, O apple tree,
In a beautiful orchard you stand,
With each long branch stretching down to the ground,
Like a fine and delicate hand.

O apple tree, O apple tree,
I watch as you grow tall,
Too big for me to reach up high,
And grab a single apple at all.

Chloe Loughran

But Where Are My Flowers?

You gave me milk chocolates
And thought I was in your powers,
You gave me a sweet card
But where are my flowers?
You gave me a weekend away
And a grand meal in the towers,
You gave me the best champagne
But where are my flowers?
You gave me an engagement ring
And a speech that lasted hours,
You gave me a white wedding
And at last I got my flowers.
You gave me two children
And love that lasts forever,
And now we do everything
Like buying flowers, together.

Stephanie Lynn Teasdale

The Seaside

I have travelled far and wide
However at the age of 53 I still love the seaside.
There are places that from the start
Always have held a special place in my Heart.
Lots of places down South
From Cornwall, Devon and Bournemouth.

Places from East and West
It's hard to say which place I like the best.
Each place is different you see
Each holds a memory for me
My favourite choice is not hard to make
Lots of years when young I spent at Ramsgate!

Making castles in the sand
Walking along the water's edge, holding my Dad's hand.
Playing games on the beach
Watching the tide going out of reach.
Going on the slot machines losing money
Buying rock tasting of honey.

Looking around for Souvenirs
Going to the pub, so Mum and Dad can have a few beers.
Wearing a 'kiss me quick' hat
Going down the slide on a mat.
Funny and view postcards to send
My second choice must be Southend!

The cliffs and the amusement arcade called Peter Pan
The longest pier in the world built by man.
These places along with others are in my past
With memories locked in my mind to last.
When worry, for a while, from my life I want to free
I just remember those lovely memories by the sea!

Joan Lipman

Dark As Night

The sky darkened just like night,
It seemed that we would need a light.
There came a flash of blinding light,
The birds disappeared and took to flight.
The rain came down it didn't stop,
And then there was an almighty drop,
Of thunder.

The noise was loud, it rumbled around,
The rain came down with a thunderous sound.
Lightning danced around the sky,
And then all of a sudden, it passed by.

We turned off the light,
The sky was nice and bright.
The rain was stopping,
The birds began to sing.
Isn't nature an incredible thing.
The storm is past, tranquillity fills the air,
Life is back to normal, no more need for despair.

Marion Lee

A Few Characters

They all are local characters
Some were ahead of their time
Yet there are a few left about
Yet still living in a time once fine.

They all are local characters
With the things they have done and said
That makes others sit and wonder
And think more about in bed.

They all are local characters
That everybody knows
For they are the backbone of this country of ours
How much we all owe to such a few.

Keith L Powell

The Driving Test

Is this your first test? My examiner inquired,
Oh. Yes, I replied and I'm truly inspired.
I've studied the manual, the Highway Code
And now I'm ready to 'hit the road'

His expression told me he wasn't impressed
He obviously didn't share my zest.
I adjusted the mirrors and fastened my belt
Euphoric describes the way that I felt

The first hundred yards went remarkably well
Until he uttered a high-pitched yell
Slow down, slow down, we're approaching a bend
Driving this way, we will both meet our end.

His face was red and his knuckles white
I've never seen such a pitiful sight
Trust me I said it's all in hand
Try to relax I'm in command

A mile or so further down the road
A rather large truck had shed its load
I manoeuvred around with incredible skill
And came to a halt on the top of a hill

My 'man' was looking a little tired
To tell the truth I thought he'd expired
We'll return to the Centre he said with a sigh
It's been a long hour for both you and I.

I sat at the wheel all flushed with success
He stepped from the car, said your driving's a mess
I hope this will be the last time we meet
So just to get even I ran over his feet

I visited him in his hospital bed
And these are the very first words that he said
I've never been so badly assailed
And I'm happy to tell you my dear that you've *failed.*

Bess Langley

Raindrops

Hanging on to leaves,
Dancing on the river,
Crouching in the grass blades,
Making them quiver.

Bringing out the perfume
So the blooms smell sweet,
Playing on umbrellas
And thumping out a beat.

Clinging to your fingers,
Sliding down your hair,
Making lashes sparkle
And looking like a tear.

Vibrant as jewels
Tumbling from the sky,
Adding life and colour
Where once the world was dry.

Gloria Thorne

The Glider

As I look out of my window
On a bright and sunny day
Across the fields where horses roam,
And farmers gather hay.

I hear a sound and look around ~
Then glance up to the sky,
A towing plane with glider
Quickly catch my eye.

I watch for several minutes ~
Until at once I see
The towrope dangling from the plane
The glider flying free.

Gracefully it dips and turns,
Catching winds so light,
A gentle swoop, then rise again
On its solo flight.

Joyce Lane

Without You

Why are the stars all crying
And the moon has faced away,
The clouds, their cloaks around me bathe
To shield the light of day.

Why has the music faded
Where have the dancers gone,
Tell them bring the curtain down
The story has been done.

Why are the shadows falling
When the sun still wants to shine,
And the stars, they still are crying
Can they hear this heart of mine.

Time waits upon the threshold
And the candles start to dim,
The light of love is leaving
Will the nightmare now begin.

Darkness falls around the room
Touched with moonlight's fond embrace,
While I reflect on tender feelings
I pray once more to see your face.

Did Angels come to me last night
And took away in sweet surrender,
All my tears and darkest dreams
Saved my soul with love so tender.

Mists of morning dawned the day
With light that stings my eyes,
While spiders drank their silver threads
Birds sang long goodbyes.

Janet Clayton

Tea For Thought

Have a cup of tea
That's what my Da always said,
Have a cup of tea
Just when things go wrong.
Warm and comforting, all is not well
Cosy and tell, what's wrong,
What's the matter, inner thoughts beat through
My brain, have another sip, O that's much better,
Thoughts flowing easier and calmer now
The smell going through all my body.
I look up, into his face 'do you want another',
That smile as he hands me another cup of Tea,
Now I know all will be well.

Marion Moylan

Life's Tapestry

Our life is a tapestry we weave,
A little every day.
What its final pattern is,
Is not for us to say.
Sometimes with hindsight
We look back and think,
Had I done that instead of this,
Or this instead of that,
Would it have made much difference?
We can't be sure of that.

The patterns that we weave each day,
We have to weave purblind,
For the patterns which we try to make
Are just shadows in our mind.
Yesterday we made mistakes,
And we'll make more today,
But is the pattern really wrong?
It is not for us to say.

We cannot see the pattern clear
That we weave every day,
The shadows and the shining bits
When the sun lights up our way.
We have to keep on weaving until the very end,
And maybe it will turn out well,
We just don't know my friend.

Valerie J Owen

My Ideal Man

Tall dark and handsome,
Is my ideal man.
They say opposites attract,
But love has no plan.

In my eyes he's perfect,
Without a single flaw.
His willingness to please,
Is something I adore.

When I look at him,
I tremble with delight.
Shivers shoot down my spine,
I love him with all my might.

As the dawn is breaking,
While wearing my night-dress,
He always says I'm beautiful,
Even though my hair's a mess!

Although we have our problems,
As many couples do.
His strength of mind and courage,
Will always see us through.

When he takes me in his arms,
He kisses me tenderly.
Nothing else seems to matter,
He's my ideal man you see!

Sandra Ann Marshall

No Answers

Footprints, large and small
Wend their way along the sandy shore.
Whose are they?
Where were they going?
Do they belong to a man or a woman?
Or to lovers walking hand in hand?
    I may never know the answers.

In a few places the tide has washed some away
Leaving large, virginal expanses of sand
Between consecutive footprints, suggesting
The persons had taken huge leaps across the sand.
Some footprints are deeper than others, why?
Did their owners stop there and look out to sea?
    I may never know the answers.

Were those who made the footprints
Hurrying along the beach to go elsewhere?
Or were they enjoying a few moments solitude
As they wandered slowly along the seashore?
Whatever the reason, they have positively left
Their mark, albeit temporarily, in the sand so golden.
    I may never know the answers.

As I walk along this very same beach
Letting my footprints mingle
With those of the persons unknown and unseen,
I realise too, that all life can be like the footprint trail,
Sometimes leading to a definite location.
While at others, it is marking time itself.
    I may never find the answer.

Paul W Fleming

A New Life

I'm in a situation I never thought I'd be,
Back to being a single girl, after years of you and me.
Yes, once we were a couple, but now we are far apart,
And when you went away from me, I know you took my heart.

But now I know it's over. We have nothing left to share,
Only the pain and sadness that both of us must bear.
Yes, a lifetime of possessions, it seems there's nothing more,
Yet I've found peace and solitude I never knew before.

There are pictures in the album, memories on every page,
But I'm living with reality. Yes wisdom comes with age
And now my heart is back with me, I can choose the path I tread
My confidence grows daily, I'm thinking with my head.

Every day as I grow stronger, I know love is everywhere.
I no longer weep or shed a tear on one who does not care.
For now I have a new life, with more meaning than before.
I've finally made a brand new start; at last I've closed the door.

Lilian Day

A Good Friend

It stands in the bedroom against the wall
We have had it before our son, now fifty, could crawl
In fact my wife has had it for sixty-two years plus a day
I hope it will keep going and not be sent away

It has served my wife well, of that I am sure
I pray it will do so for many times more
It has been through thick and thin to complete its task
Done the impossible and all that one could ask

I have seen her use it, amongst her many chores
With her head down, for hours without pause
The items that she has made in the years gone by
If piled up would reach far up into the sky

It's made all the curtains for our home
Made bicycle saddles of leather to cover foam
Repaired sheets, made a cushion for the cat
Even put the tail on a Davey Crockett hat

It's cast and black, old fashioned but strong
That's the reason it's been working so well for so long
No little dials or plastic parts are to be seen
Of course you guessed, it's the wife's Singer machine

John Nelson

Paddy's One True Love

When the fields are white with daisies,
I shall return to you,
Yes long ago, these words were said,
And soon they will come true.

When the fields are white with daisies,
I will return once more,
To see my one true love,
And hold her close once more.

When the fields are white with daisies
Your Paddy will return,
Yes home again to Hornchurch,
Is what my heart does yearn.

When the fields are white with daisies
I shall return to you,
And never will we ever part,
For my love is true to you.

Anthony K Philpot

High-Rise Neighbour

My neighbour ~
who is he?
A faceless blur
exchanging greetings
on the morning air.
I cannot now recall
his name,
the colour of his eyes,
his hair.
We have lived side by side
for twenty years ~
or is it more?
Butterflies flitting silently
from the chrysalides
on the fifteenth floor.
We did speak, once
in the public gardens,
several sentences passed:
we talked of roses, aphids,
the drudgery of mowing grass.
But that was several
summers
since then the time has flown;
Now in-between the silences
the barriers have
grown.

Emelie Buckner

My Thoughts!

I'm in a place of death,
I'm in a place of life.
I'm in a place of happiness,
Where there's much strife.
I'm in a place that screams black,
I'm in a place whispering white.
I'm in a place never wrong,
Which is also never right.
I'm in a place filled with tears,
I'm in a place with much laughter.
I'm in a place with no future,
With a happy ever after.
I'm in a place full of love,
I'm in a place of unkind.
Have you guessed it yet?
I'm in your mind.

Marianne White

Carpet Maker

Like the myriad strands of silk
Used by the Turkish carpet makers
Thoughts run side by side in my mind
Competing for prominence
Each coloured differently
But contributing
To the detailed, intricate pattern
Of my life

Like an unfinished carpet
In which only God knows
The pattern which is slowly unfolding
Each stitch painstakingly and skilfully sewn
As life's experiences blend together
To form the whole picture.

Will I like this carpet when it's finished?
Each part interwoven
Like the warp and weft
Sometimes going in one direction
And sometimes another.

There are imperfections if you look closely
But when you step back
And see the full effect
The overall creation reflects the clever design
And the skilled craftsmanship at work.

Christine Laverock

A Magnetic Charm

I once saw a great Russian owl
In the middle of a busy shopping mall.
I wondered what he was thinking,
Just sitting on his perch blinking.
Such a stunning sight
One could have watched
Him all night.
With charming splendour,
An owl so alone
Many many miles
From his home.

Janet Weatherhead

Generosity

It was hinted, but with clarity
Something exciting, be done for charity
Happy, carefree, feeling good
Promptly indicated, definitely would
Climbing up high, free and easy
Suddenly the stomach's getting queasy
Now thinking, of things unkind
Untold fear, gripping the mind
Sitting there, with adrenaline rising
All up tight, it's not surprising
Fixing the harness, specially adjusted
Cast iron safe, tried and trusted
Over the edge, must be insane
Never, never, never, ever again
Gasping for breath, trying to cope
On the end of a bungee rope

A W Day

The Blot

The steel frame grow with no time to waste
you could see at a glance it would leave a bad taste,
for it seemed to bend and twist as it rose
like an angry wart on a witch's nose.

For this was an architect's pride and joy
like a child he'd play with his brand new toy,
a true wonder, fantastic, the perfect dream
but one guaranteed to make the locals scream.

So what if, some of them kicked up a fuss
or brought in the greens on a flower powered bus,
just let one of them climb a single tree
we'll chop it from under um; just you see.

For this was no ordinary run of the mill blot
environmentally the cost would be ever such a lot,
with no way to stop it, once construction begun
this carbuncle would become, second to none.

And if that wasn't enough, for the locals to endure
the planners came to break, the very last straw,
we've thought of a name, said the evil fiends
and so it was called, Milton Keynes.

J R Hirst

Evensong ~ Winchester Cathedral

There across from where I sat,
Still after centuries of devout format;
High on a shelf spaced alone,
King Canute's bone encased in stone.

Across from where I sat,
The walls echo their magnificat,
And exude a distillate mist;
With the devoted past we emphemerally tryst.

Late afternoon does a peace bestow,
In the light of candle glow,
And in choir psalm and Placido;
While evening words into vastness and shadow go.

Mighty Danish lord, a pagan firebrand,
Came to accept other values and a restraining hand;
Some flatterers goaded him to disagree,
Had to prove his limit over the sea.

Through years he has listened with patient grace,
From his final resting place;
In Latin, English, and changing dialect,
And centuries of superficial fashion subject.

What now does he have to say,
To us in our very advanced way
So far removed from his awesome day;
Is there a message that still holds sway?

Know the waters and study well,
The tide will not be denied its high swell;
Yet pray to change all things right,
To forward and intensify the progressive light.

The inevitability of change does not forget the past,
It carries with it the things that will last,
An enduring spirit survives, long since begot;
There across from where I sat.

   Eric Ashwell

Only To Be With You

to see your face
to feel your touch
to kiss your lips
to hold your hand
to stroke your hair
to look into your eyes
to make you smile
to hear your voice
to be in your dreams
to share our love
to wake up with you
only to be with you

    Leisha

The Face

The face reflects the pain
Of years of tormented neglect,
The face that reminds again
Of the social war effect.

The face of human suffering
This hell has brought for years,
The face that anger's covering
To fight away the tears.

The face that has no memories
Of life before the pain,
The face that hates its enemies,
The face that reminds again.

The face that makes us wonder
Of how it used to be,
The face with looks of thunder,
The face that cannot see.

The face is mine and yours now,
The face of tempers worn,
The face is mine and yours, how
Where memories born?

Marcus Tyler

Jessica

How could words alone explain
The beauty of the moon and stars
Could verse begin to tell of a perfect summer's day
Or could your thoughts contain the creation of earth
Actions would never tell of what's in your mind's eye
As speech will never tell of your love that will never die
You could only sum up parts of your life in a book
We only know parts of the past and present
Nothing of the future
As with the mysteries of the universe
I can't explain in words or actions how perfect you are to me.

A Griffin

Village Dreams

She sat at the bus stop,
On the old seat,
All day.
Remembering the times
The buses passed
That way.

The village once so proud,
A great asset
Had been.
But a supermarket
Sadly replaced
The green.

No kindly voices now,
Strangers walking
Her street.
Friends were long dead leaving
Just echoes of
Their feet.

The day had such promise,
Reliving dreams
She'd said.
Now dreams of her village
Were best kept in
Her head.

Angela Pritchard

To Spring

A friendly glow that touches all
Whilst winds outside do blow
Comes from the brightly burnished coal
That warms from head to toe

The burning logs that crack and spit
An eerie spell transpires
The only light are candles lit
Their flames dance if on wires

A warming drink to melt the chill
As rain beats out the time
Against the panes and windowsill
You ponder warmer climes

A lazy thought before you drowse
Comes to your weary brain
Soon will be done they'll lift the clouds
And winter will be gone

When spring burst forth with life anew
The buds, the trees start showing
Full of new leaves and flowers too
Burst forth with pride so glowing

So think of this as now you sit
With feelings sad and wistful
As very soon this time will flit
And life once more be blissful

Trev Taylor

The Awakening

Maybe it will snow soon
When grey clouds cloak the moon
Softly like pure white stars, crystal gleaming on their way.
Trails of frosted teardrops clustering upon the ground
Do heaven's daughters descend
Upon the still rock iron earth.
This is now the time of birth
When seeds will swell in the shrouded earth
This is the time of silent sleep when creatures
Of the warm sunlight hide away in places
Dark, and do not wake till summer calls them
To arise and stretch their sleep-worn limbs
When the world greets their awakenings.

Pamela Gamell

Perfect Melody

From the dainty little Daisy, like diamond dew upon the green
To the tallest giant Sunflower the world has ever seen.
Or the brightly shining Buttercup along the side hedgerow
To the beautiful blue of the Eidelweiss sparkling in the snow.

The tiny Scarlet Pimpernel fluttering on the leas
With Heartsease close beside it stout against the breeze.
The Harebells lazy swaying in the warm and Summer air
Bright Celandines, Convolvulus and Birds Eye everywhere.

Vibrant Poppies gleaming amidst the golden corn
With sea-blue Cornflowers blooming as newly comes the dawn.
The shy purple Slipper Orchids or the pure Star of Bethlehem
Wild flowers are Nature's Wonder, the World's most gentle gems.

Wild Roses on the hedgerows, Sea Thrift upon the dune,
Flowers are like a melody, to bring our hearts in tune!

    Mollie D Earl

For A Son Killed In A Car Crash

As larks and the shy sea-lavender steal across
the marsh Mac splash-cools himself in the dikes;
on mud-dry paths oyster-catchers and song
are everywhere on the dog's path. Soft breezes
rise out of the barley fields, stirring the air;
wild flowers in plenty ring round the coastal path.

White horses gallop over the strand; brown
sails, hard by, bear the heart high; curlews call;
heron and whimbrel haunt; and as I step
gingerly along frail planks, razor-bills shriek.
'Be off,' they say. Mac and I choose to ignore them
and make for the sea and wet sand, rack weed and waders.

Oh, the world is a tumult of glorying sight and sound,
of enthralling object and tangled subject, as yours
was too my too-much-loved son. Let's sing as cuckoos
and nightingales do this early summer. Hark!

Murmur we
names as a monk on his rosary counts, or
a mother fingers o'er her bairn's wee pinkies. Fathers
too, like you, of a night linger the tale at bedtime out.
Thus you freed their fancies, each safe in the love of a fearless
creation. It was just such a spell that you cast, my son.

Yet your time was: ours is perforce. The dark
though, is charged with such pure loving light:
as my dog and I turn from the stark
gloom, I find everywhere bright
hope and gifts such as you gave, my son.

John K Coleridge

Meeting Of The Minds

I wish I were the summer sun
that I may kiss your skin.
I yearn to hold you in my arms
and warm your heart within.

I wish I were the cool night breeze
free to move without a care.
I long to be there with you now
and gently touch your hair.

I wish I were the sight and sounds
that arouse your searching mind.
I hope you come to realise
that we're really two of a kind.

I sense we are of similar ilk
and on convergent lines.
That our paths will one day cross
is there in all the signs.

Philip Newton

Reflections

Hand that ripples in the water
Swaying to feel its touch,
Smooth and soft,
Cool and yet warm to the touch
I take my hand out,
To watch the drops, like pearl drops,
Falling back to where they came
The touch so beautiful.
I look to see my reflection
Like a great big mirror,
I smile as I watch, the ripples of my touch.

Laura Stinchcombe-Sorrell

The Unappreciated Friend

I had never been so angered so easily
By someone so incredibly fake,
Until the day I knew that, feasibly,
I had a heart you could break.

I understood little, or nothing
Or anything you had to say.
I understand little or nothing,
And you're standing in my way.

The demons inside your skull
Are undeniably there,
Clouding your vision of me,
And that's desperately unfair.

And it's not that you wouldn't say it,
That February's still here,
Not like you couldn't understand it,
The basis of all of my fear.

It was just that you couldn't portray it,
The sympathy that you felt,
As deep inside of my heart,
The ice queen was starting to melt.

And as much as I saw I was hurting you
When I took out the anger I felt,
You were fast boring me,
Into a hypochondriacs hell.

The only good place for you, is out of my life,
Go! Wallow in all of your pain!
But I know that since gaining and losing you,
I will never be quite the same.

Laura Susan Arnold

Homesick

Sealed behind the glass am I.
'Infectious' am I.
Through my huge inky eyes, people I see.
Wearing masks over mouths are they.
Press my hands on the glass to watch, do I.
Stick and make smudges do they. Make patterns do I!

Weak am I. Spirit low, like long cape dragging on the floor, it is.
Sad, so sad am I. Cry and cry do I.
People understand? Not they. Object for prodding am I.
Naked and cold in soul and in life, am I.

Man speak. Listen hard, do I.
'Kill.' Say he. 'Kill now.'
'Now!' Say kind lady in white coat. 'No! Live should he. Life is he.'

Sad am I. People not understand.
Life is me. Love I bring.
Hate they give. Fear they show.

Not kind lady.
Kind lady bring love, but bad man afraid.
Dead, they want I. Home I want. Home I need.
Escape . . . cannot. I sealed behind glass.
Die here, will I.
I alien, with skin of scale and pure of white.
Trapped on Earth am I, never go home.
Sad, oh so sad, for people so afraid and hating of little me.
Never love and reach out to me.
The one to speak for all the peoples, am I.
Earth, island in space, now and forever.

And die here, will I. For nothing.

Leonie Smith

Journeys

Nothing to look at, nothing to see
The journey commences
I wish it's not me.

I've done it before, I'll do it again
And just as before
I wish it won't be.

It's dark outside as black as can be
And the worst thing of all
Through the window it's *me*.

The coffee's run out, the Flap Jack is gone
My mouth is so dry
I wish it not be.

I look at my watch, the time hasn't moved
Since I stood on the platform
And lost one of my shoes.

It fell on the track twix the train and me
I stood there agape
Till staff rescued me.

Along they came with pole and hook
Smiling, nudging and gleeful look
My face turned red, I lowered my head
And wished like hell it just wasn't me.

At last it seems the end's in sight
My thoughts turn to the one who waits
Excitement rises, warm thoughts and feelings
Just can't wait for journey's ending.

J Bowman

War-Time Memories

I was quite young at the height of the war,
When this happened, I was only four.
This was life, I only knew this way,
I'd never known peace, not one single day.

The aircraft are coming, they're flying low,
There's only now, one place to go.
Run for shelter as fast as you can,
Hide away from the nasty man.

Now wait a minute, hold on a sec',
My playthings are littered all over the deck.
What should I do, I can't leave them there,
These are my things for which I care.

I ran out again to rescue my treasure,
These simple things give me great pleasure.
Amid all the shouting, amid all the noise,
Hitler won't bomb my precious toys.

Michael Dennis

The Beauty Of Islay

For Islay's own beauty
Is beckoning to me
Over mountains and valleys
Across the wide sea
Wind in the clouds white
Chasing rain everywhere
The birds will be singing
On my Islay so fair

Those birds on my island
They spin not nor sow
For God in His mercy
Provides there below
Wind in the clouds white
Chasing rain everywhere
And birds will be singing
On that sanctuary so fair

Yes Islay's own beauty
Where God's peace is strong
Harmonious nature
The wildlife in song
Wind in the clouds white
Chasing rain everywhere
For God gave us Islay
My Islay so fair

Mary Hudson

Little Robin Redbreast

Lonely little Robin, perched upon the tree,
Come and share a little bread,
And keep me company,
Come sit upon my windowsill,
And sing a little song,
To brighten up my dreary day,
And help me get along.

Soon it will be Christmas, and snow upon the ground,
I'll save some crumbs and nuts for you,
If you will stay around,
How nice 'twill be, to have a friend,
To come and call on me,
My little Robin Redbreast,
Who sits upon my tree.

Annie McKimmie

Afternoon Tea

A pleasant trip to visit the Dales
A nice Tea Room when it's time for tea
White lace cloths and china cups
It's really a pleasure to see

Chintz curtains at the windows
Matching covers on chairs
Small flower arrangements decorating tables
Sideboards displaying their wares

Warm fluffy scones with jam and cream
Floral china pot of tea
Small fancy cakes on a cakestand
All set out to tempt me

Then perhaps a slice of fruit cake
Or a piece of apple pie
Everything home-baked and tasty
All displayed to please the eye

A perfect way to end the day
As you relax in this friendly place
Time seems to stand still for a moment
The experience brings a smile to your face

In these busy days of hustle and bustle
With TV meals on a tray
It's nice to go back to the old ways
And eat in a leisurely way

Peggy Hunter

The Sleepers

Buried deep within the earth
In the country of their birth
Lay the dead of ancient wars
Sacrificed for many a cause.

Over moor and over valley
Long-forgotten warriors lie
Roman, Celt and Norman noble
All in anonymity.

Men of Lancaster and York
Pike and bowmen, young and old
Left behind their grieving loved ones
To perish on the snowy wold.

Puritan and Cavalier, in the fusel's deadly hail.
Faced the cannon's belching muzzle
All were buried where they fell.

Centuries of conflict
Stained our land with human blood
Faceless victims long forgotten
Buried deep in field and wood.

As you walk our country byways
See the sun on roof and spire
Hear the lark sing in the heavens
Soaring ever higher and higher.

Woolly sheep graze in the meadows
As they have done from ancient time
Such a scene of rural beauty
Gives a sense of peace sublime.

Passing time has cleansed the landscape
Every trace of strife is gone
Deep within their secret places
Silent sleepers slumber on.

Janet Cavill

The Sky

In the mornings I like to look at the sky,
I just do, I don't know why,
What amazes me, this is quite true,
Is that the sky is always blue.

You may think that the night sky is black,
But may I just explain this back,
That sky isn't black, that's just old lark,
You see, it's blue but very dark.

Nicola Avino (14)

The Millennium

The Millennium could be a chance
To show just how we care
For these beloved isles of ours
These acres ~ dear and fair
Can we get back our pride of race
To dare and fight and win
To keep our heritage intact
Our morals free from sin?
We've lost all pride in Britain's code
Of goodness and fair play
Can we get back our pride and joy?
So other lands will say
'Britannia's waking up again
We'd better toe the line
She's apt to gird her loins again
She's showing every sign
Of putting back the *Great* before
The Britain that we know
And showing us how we should behave
To all who wish to sow'
The seeds of love and brotherhood,
Help for the poor and sad,
A yearning for a time of peace,
For every lass and lad

Ethel M Crowther

Sands Of Time

They walked together along the sand
A loving couple hand in hand
All worries they had left behind
They were in love it didn't mind

In another world they called their own
They lived together like Darby and Joan
Just for today they'd come to see
Where they were young and fancy free

Recalling memories from the past
There they were, together at last
Free from suffering, free from pain
Never to be apart again

They slowly disappeared from sight
Into the darkness of the night
This loving couple hand in hand
Left no footprints in the sand.

Edith M Stott

Earth's Jewels

If you look around you from the sky to the ground,
You will find a myriad of colours 'abound'
The roses are red, the sky is blue,
And there are many kinds of hue.

An artist's palette,
Is made up of such things
And they can make a painting sing.

The colours of a storm,
Can make you feel scary,
They put you on the alert
And make you more wary.

But after a storm the clouds glow
These are known as a rainbow
The sunsets of multicoloured hue
Can bring happiness to me and you.

Without such colours our lives would be drab
And we would go around dejected and sad.
So thank the Lord for being so good
Without his help we would look like mud.

Dorothy Morris-Hague

Mum's Eye View

My daughter is a lovely girl
From a mum's eye view you see
Just like her dad in every way
Not one bit like me.
A double act one might say
Dad shines through on every score
As she is growing day by day
I see him more and more.
Happy in her toddling ways
Gay, bright and full of verve
Darting here and darting there
'Oh baby watch that kerb.'
Teaching her the do's and don'ts
It does become a skill
Then I worry day by day
Until at night she's still.
Time goes by so quickly
I look at her in wonder,
A graceful lady doth appear
By jove, who steals the thunder.
Altered slightly in her looks
A little more like me
My daughter is a lovely girl
From a mum's eye view you see.

Dorothy Knight

The Wonders Of My World

The air that I breath
The blue sky above my head
The clouds up above all fluffy and white
And when the sun has gone
The stars at night

What I wonder
Keeps the stars so high and bright
I wonder who wakes the sun early in the morn
Who tells the birds to sing at dawn
Who tells the flowers to put on their best
Sparkling nature's own treasure chest

The buzzing of the bees as they go from flower to flower
And the thirsty earth welcomes the daytime shower

The love of a four-legged friend
The trusting love of a new-born babe
The love of a brother for a sister
The love of a miss for a mister
All these wonders so plain to see
Belong to you and me
Wonderful, wonderful world.

Marilyn Campbell

Roses

The symbol of Lancashire is a red, red rose
With a perfume oh so sweet,
But when the county's folk sit down to dine,
Many odd things they do eat.
A strange concoction, they call hotpot
Is made with potatoes, onions and lamb,
Sometimes they soak dried peas
Then cook them with a pestle of ham.
Black puddings made with oats and blood
As a starter or breakfast treat,
Mashed up spuds with steak and cowheel,
Which really are cows' feet!
Tripe with salt, pepper and vinegar or
With onions cooked in milk,
They say it doesn't need chewing and
Slips down as smooth as silk.
Fish and chips with mushy peas
Washed down with tea in a mug,
Jam butties, bread and butter pudding
With custard served in a jug.
All these things belong to Lancs, but when it's
Time for a Sunday joint,
The tradition of the adjoining county
Then they do appoint,
Roast beef with Yorkshire pudding and onion gravy
Is their treat,
Rice pudding served as afters
Is a meal you cannot beat!

John Kirkham

Marking Time

When you get old (what's old!) well, older,
And the summers get shorter and winters colder,
Each day must be stretched as far as 'twill go,
The brain activated, the blood made to flow.
Stimulate memory and sharpen the sight.
Don't vacillate with what's wrong and what's right.
Each cell must be incited to work.
Pushed to the limit. There's no time to shirk.
Fresh books to be read. Strange words to be found.
Ears tuned in to listen for every new sound.
No chance to be lost. No stone left unturned.
No ventures rejected or outings adjourned.
We none of us know the length of life's span
So get out and live it as long as you can.

Mollie Wade

Seasons Of Life

Memories a river rambling waves of thought
Thoughts like leaves drifting into our mind
Mind the whirlpool on which we rely
The voice the author of our thoughts
Thoughts the key to our soul.

The soul the key to our remembrance
Our lives like the seasons forever unfold
Mine is the winter to behold
Roaming the land of my past
I see the true meaning of me at last.

The last breath of the icy winter grips
My soul
We exist don't we
I turn and I am in the spring time
My journey begins
I am reborn.

Christine A Smithies

Dead To Sleep

Flaming nova
blasts the stars out of the sky
makes the fellwalkers' hike a dream
to stop
heavy boots
thudding clouded monocled plinths
breath slimed in fulsome deep

torching singeing candleswoon
clocks the moths
midge-bitten thumbs
miles throbbing stools of feet
working the blackgreen hours till they were dead
the hand of the man loved and held
brief cataclysm swooping
sunk-ridge valley
sucking legs and steeping cries

caved rocks raindrummed pillows of ice
torn brick-worn muddied foot-pools
inching death by a mouldy woodrotten stump
swallowing lidded knees where it leaves the flesh
of a barnacled cleft-hidden kiss-print
fingers

tearing at the years as though they would never wake

Julie Ashpool

A Bad Day

When I opened the curtains, I was blinded
By a blanket of snow on the ground
It'll take ages to start the car
Oh! No! I'd forgotten! It's in the pound!

They towed it from outside the pub yesterday
It's unroadworthy, whatever that means
It's got a roof, four doors, an engine
Gear lever, and five wheels!

The tyres are bald, I grant you
But there's nothing badly wrong
Now I'll have to catch a bus to work
It'll take me twice as long!

Of course, they'll have noticed the front of the car's
Bashed in, I crashed into a wall for a bet
(I was drunk at the time) and it's certain they'll
Know the tax hasn't been renewed yet!

I know the boot door's wonky
It doesn't fasten properly
And I tied the exhaust to the car with string
But it works all right for me!

Well, that's it, I can't have the car back
They said it's a lump of lead
And there's only one place for an ancient wreck
I'm ~ going back to bed!

Anne Wareing

Change

Everything keeps on changing
Nothing stays the same
The old days were the best ones
Or so most people claim

What happened to the shilling
Now there's only pounds and pence
And these don't seem to go so far
It doesn't make much sense

And where are bus conductors now
They used to take our fare
Now drivers undertake their jobs
Alone instead of in a pair

In the shops it's all self-service
The choice is never-ending
We fill our trolleys then queue up
To find we're overspending

And are there still twenty-four hours each day
Because in times gone by
The days were so much longer then
But now they seem to fly

All this change is so confusing
It's like some sort of game
Waiting just to catch us out
Nothing stays the same.

Vivien Holden

Noises In The Night

Noises in the night like the creaking on the stairs
Is there an intruder, or is it a nightmare
I slip out of bed and creep down the stairs,
And when I reach the hall I call out 'Who's there?'
Then I hear a meow and looking at the mat
There as bold as brass is a neighbour's cat
How did he get in, what is he doing there?
Then in the lounge I notice hairs upon a chair
Was this the first time or has he done it before
How did he get in, why through the cat flap on the door
It was there for my cat who died last May
And I forgot to remove or secure it some way.

Diana Daley

Fish And Chips

The chips are crisp and nice to taste.
The fish in golden batter.
If you consume too much of them
They say you'll get much fatter.

But fish and chips in moderation
Will do us no harm.
There's no better sight wrapped up in paper
And mounted in my palm.

With a touch of salt and vinegar
And a buttered muffin besides,
A wholesome feast of protein
This simple dish provides.

The neon light is now diffused
The chippy serves no more,
Until they turn the open sign
Tomorrow at half past four.

Neville Anthony

My Monkey

I've got a monkey living with me ~
He doesn't live up a tree!
He's brown, soft and cuddly
When I am naughty,
He takes the blame
Even though ~ it's a shame!
My Nan will talk to him on the phone ~
When I want to be left alone.
But when I go to school, he'll have to stay at home ~ that's the rule!
He can keep my mom safe and sound ~
Until once more I'm around
Come on Mr Monkey time for bed
There's still a story to be read.

Sylvia Jennings

Spring

Flowers blooming in the breeze,
Birds chirping in the trees,
Rivers flowing clear and clean,
Many meadows lush and green.

The sun is shining yet the day is cold,
The joy of spring cannot be sold.
The great outdoors is at its best
And nature's work is at the test.

Daffodils flowering in the Spring,
Whistling its tune the wind will sing.
When the sun goes down and out of sight
Foxes leap into the night.

Gemma King

Sidmouth

A tea room, on a summer's day
With little time to share
A pot of tea, and happy talk,
And scrumptious bill of fare.

A repast in a pleasant room
Too soon, the time to part.
But on another summer's day,
This thought will tug my heart.

   Amelia Wilson

Impression of St Giles's Church, Cambridge

Sun shafts through high leaded windows
filling lofty belfried heights,
bathing the sandstone pillars in golds;
warmth-exuding mellowness unfolds
space and room.

Organ music gently rising
touching, livening, wood-beamed roof,
flowing round the columns solid,
running up each archway stolid
dispelling gloom.

While stained glass saints look on benignly,
parishioners join in happy gathering;
laughing, listening, freely fuse,
unhampered by rows of stiffening pews
or ancient stone tomb.

Helen M Seeley

Own Bed

Tonight you're in your own bed
I've been waiting ages for this
No more pushing and poking me
Tonight should be quite bliss.

No more pinching the blankets
Or arms wrapped round my head
No more nattering till all hours
At last you're in your bed.

But no more kisses and cuddles
No bedtime stories to share
I'm missing your warm little body
Oh . . . I'd rather you back in here!

Sarah J Bell

Runaway

Sitting on the pavement
With her clothes inside a bag
Asking passers-by for money,
Food or just a fag
Selling her body twice nightly
For drugs to numb the pain
And when she needs another fix
She'll just walk the streets again
Dirty, cold and hungry
No place to sleep at night
The same yesterday, tomorrow
There seems no end in sight
It never used to be this way
She was a girl without a care
But abuse has left her damaged
That child's no longer there
She doesn't really want for much
Just somewhere safe to stay
Now she's just another statistic
Yet another runaway

Wendy Trott

Kids

You pick them up,
And hold them up
To get their little windies up.

You feed them up,
And dress them up
Then do your best to bring them up.

You do them up,
And lace them up
And very often shut them up.

Sometimes you feel you could tie them up,
There comes a time when you give them up.
But you never, ever let them down.

D Tinson

Staple Plain

Nestled between the Quantock Hills,
Above the cove ~ St Audrey's Bay;
A little piece of heaven lies ~
A place to spend a peaceful day.

Through the gateway, down the track,
A marvellous scene will come in sight;
Past sitkas, beeches, oak and ash ~
Infinite bliss to left and right.

By tall protectors of the wood,
Their boughs saluting row by row,
In sympathetic harmony
The gorse bush blooms below.

In May the rhododendrons flower,
Majestic in their sprawling stance;
With myriad purple trumpets clothe
Deserving more than casual glance.

Hills spread out beyond the paths
Imbued with secrets never told;
Beckoning to be explored ~
What bygone memories do they hold?

Veiled hills of mystery like the dusk ~
Their garments stone and bracken green;
May they for generations stay
Unspoilt, enhancing every scene.

A quiet, tranquil paradise
To feed the soul and still the mind;
Serenity in every view ~
Nature, indeed, is wondrous kind.

Mary Farrell

Life Blood Of Our City

Between seven hills a river gently winds
Refreshing the land and bringing joy to me ~
A peace, a stillness and a place to stand and stare:-
For water is the life blood of the city.

Under seven hills a river quietly flows
Bubbling into springs, with heat of high degree.
That made this place into a healing spa:-
For water is the life blood of the city!

Leading from the seven hills man has now built
His own small river, required for industry
But now reopened as a place for pleasure:-
For water is the life blood of the city.

In Bath, city of the seven hills, we enjoy
Water in abundance, and outpoured bounty,
To drink, to wash, to use for work and for play:-
For water is the life blood of the city!

M E Weeks

Simple Pleasures

Looking back on childhood days
    Many years ago
TV had not been heard of
    But we had a radio

On holidays and at weekends
    What did we do for leisure
Skipping ~ hopscotch ~ hide and seek
    All these gave us pleasure

Sometimes we'd pack a picnic
    On a lovely sunny day
Then eat it in the garden
    We seldom went away

The old familiar cry today
    Is ~ Mum what can we do
In spite of their expensive toys
    They still want something new

So looking back I still can say
    My childhood days were fun
Simple pleasures ~ many friends
    Yes ~ happy days each one.

P E Poole

Paraphrase For Ann

Based on a sonnet by Shakespeare that described his lady, warts and all

My Darling's eyes are bright as any sun,
And coral's red tones well with her lips' red.
Her breasts have curves no Fragonard would shun,
And soft brown hair adorns her lovely head.
I've seen fine banks of roses, pink and white,
But none outshine the roses in her cheeks:
Her style of dressing fills me with delight;
Beside her model-girls might look like freaks.
I love to hear her speak, for well I know
That music never has a sweeter sound.
I have no need to see a goddess go
My love, when she walks out, treads on firm ground.
She is, indeed, so elegant and rare
No others do I see that can compare.

F Littlewood

puddles

puddles are rain from the sky
gathered into pools
not to be walking in
those are my parents rules
but, puddles are for stamping in,
puddles are for fun
puddles are for getting wet
and wetting everyone.

Tom Sage